To Fonty —
You are dear to me —
very special.
Love,
Jan

HOMELAND

HOMELAND

Essays Beside and Beyond the Rio Grande

JAN EPTON SEALE

NEW SANTANDER PRESS

New Santander Press
P. O. Box 306
Edinburg, Texas 78540

ISBN 0-935071-10-5

Illustration, cover & book design: Erren Seale

for
Bob Sherman
world-class friend

Contents

In Sight of The Rio Grande

INLAND TERRITORY

ACKNOWLEDGEMENTS

The author gratefully acknowledges permission from the following sources to reprint:

Texas Monthly for "Remembering the Sabbath"

Universal Family for "A Bird? A Plane? An Aviophobe!"

riverSedge for "Safe"

Southwestern American Literature for "One Day in the Life of a South Texas Juror"

The Monitor (McAllen) for "Life As We Know It" and versions of "The Pursuit of Happiness," "Taking the Heat Off the Valley," "And the Rocket's Red Glare," "Hometown," and "Recognizing Freedom"

The Corpus Christi Caller-Times for "Palm Reading," "Just Bill Me," "Taking a Run at Joggers," "It's Time for the Doldrums," and "Letter to a Long-ago Boy"

The Town Crier for "Garlic and Other Children," "Getting It Together at Falcon," and "Sepia Print"

The Valley Land Fund Newsletter for "The Possible Possum."

Thanks to Kathlyn Egbert, Al Ramirez, and Erren Seale for editorial and design help.

In Sight Of
The Rio Grande

Life As We Know It

At first I blended the sound with the dream I was having, this sound of singing voices accompanied by soft guitars. But the music went on and on, so I woke up to investigate. There on my porch, at 2 a.m. on Mother's Day, was a group of my university students serenading this *mamacita gringa* with songs of appreciation and love. I was hopelessly hooked that night in 1977.

It's a phenomenon that doesn't get much press, this internalizing by Anglos of Hispanic culture. Maybe to mention it is not p.c. (politically correct), as in the condescending "Some of my best friends are Hispanic/Anglo/Fill-in-the-blank." But the term "American Melting Pot" works both ways. In soup, the potatoes take on the flavor of carrots, the tomatoes redden the chicken broth, the onions lend their savor to all.

One of my Anglo friends said recently that she and her husband had tried to move to Hawaii but they discovered they couldn't do without Tex-Mex food and music longer than a week so they guessed they'd stay in the Rio Grande Valley.

Another one said she was glad our university was getting a doctoral program in her area because she wanted to continue her studies but couldn't bear to leave Valley culture.

I asked a couple of single people who eat out all the time if they ate Mexican food often. The Anglo of the two replied, "Food IS Mexican food." And the other day I noticed that my weekly grocery list has come to include tortillas.

But it's more than food. A rootless highly mobile generation may find Hispanic family closeness enviable. Last week a man in our neighborhood showed me a picture of his granddaughter on her first birthday. "We had a huge fiesta for her on Sunday—a piñata, cookout, all the relatives from all over." He looked down at the little thing in her ribbons and lace and laughed indulgently. "She didn't give a hoot about it but the rest of us had a great time!"

Pardon me, but could I borrow that sense of celebration, that joy of living that calls into play all sorts of excuses for getting together with friends and family? I'd like to graft it on to my logical Puritan work ethic which mandates a reason, and a darned good one, to put aside our serious work in the interest of rest, fun, and familial cohesion.

When I'm traveling and start home via Houston, finally getting to that gate marked "Rio Grande Valley" and on that plane headed south, when I see all those dark-haired heads in rows in front of me, when I hear only Spanish (well...a little Japanese and

Chinese lately), when people are saying *"Perdón!"* and *"Por favor"* and smiling, I relax. I'm tired, from where I've just come from, of rude motorists, shoving opportunists, hotfooters and hustlers. It's a relief to be on this plane. I'm finally with my people and I'm going home. Never mind that I'm a *bolilla*, a biscuit face. (Don't *you* call me that—it wouldn't be p.c.)

The dictionary has two definitions for "acculturation": 1) the process of adopting the cultural traits or social patterns of another group, and 2) a restructuring or blending of cultures resulting from this. The first definition is what all of us who live here in the Rio Grande Valley of Texas together do on a personal level, in subtle or not so subtle ways, whether we will it or not. The second is the social result, in our case this unique land called The Valley.

Trinidad Gonzales, a reporter for the McAllen *Monitor*, told in a column about the burial of his Uncle Julian, a *vaquero* on the Laguna Seca Ranch north of Edinburg. Trinidad mused that his hopes for his larger Valley family included their continued listening to the past, and their maintaining a sense of self in the face of unproven "progress." Sound words for a land shifting beneath our feet.

Can I have those things too, Trinidad? I'll add them to Valley food, people, and customs that I've come to cherish.

TAKING THE HEAT OFF THE VALLEY

Tell someone upstate you're from the Valley and they make a sound like they've just been hooked up to a respirator. "Oh, the Valley! It's so hot down there!" While you're wetting your lips for a mild remonstrance, they add by way of apology, "Of course, it's the humidity. How do you *stand* it?"

If they don't faint altogether from this one-sided free-associating, you try to get across a basic tenet: The Valley is not any hotter or any more humid than much of the rest of Texas. And a basic corollary: Living in the sub-tropics is not exactly exile on Elba.

The National Weather Service at Brownsville reports a relative mean humidity of 76 percent. Compare this to Corpus Christi and Houston at 77 percent, Galveston at 78 percent, and Dallas, Austin and San Antonio at 67 percent. It's only when you get to Amarillo, at 55 percent, or El Paso, at 39 percent, that you have to worry about flaky scalp.

Okay, okay, it's *somewhat* humid in the Valley.

So shoes in the back of the closet get a little cradle cap, and mushrooms have been known to sprout indoors on carpets. We're not spending a minute bemoaning the fate of people who ask for a *sheet* of stamps at the p.o. instead of a book or roll, or who leave the sack open all night and are surprised that the chips taste like oak leaves the next morning.

We never gave the heat or humidity a second thought until someone invented the dreaded Heat Index. Now, if the thermometer reading is 90 degrees and the humidity is 85 percent, we go around martyred, telling ourselves we're enduring 117 degree heat. Only when 90 degrees meets up with a relative humidity of 30 percent—probably some July day at noon three miles east of El Paso— is it *really* 90 degrees.

And how did the Valley draw a bum rap on heat-via-humidity? In my scientific search for the definitive answer, I asked meteorologist forecaster Don Ocker of the National Weather Service in Brownsville. "I don't know," he said. "People are much better off here than in New Orleans or Memphis. I've had humidity condense on my ears when I stepped outdoors in New Orleans at night." So much for scientific documentation.

Ocker says Washington has not invented a heat index that includes wind. If they do, the Valley will be sitting pretty because a sea breeze at about 12 mph sweeps across us daily during the summer. (That's why the Deep South lost the Civil War—no breeze.)

He concedes the lush vegetation in the Valley could account for a little more moisture since green

plants give off water. Some people think the irrigation canals contribute to the humid feeling in the air,
but that's iffy. Elevation, or rather lack of it, could
figure. The Lower Rio Grande Valley averages 20
feet above sea level, give or take an anthill or Indian
mound. So any wind blowing directionally from the
south, west, or northwest will be a downhill wind to
the Valley, and such a wind creates pressure and thus
heats the air like a heat pump.

Personally I think the Valley's had bad press.
Someone says, "Whoo–eee! That hot ol' Valley!" and
it's repeated like a junior high game of Gossip.
McAllen often takes the dubious honor of "hot spot
in the nation" but that's more likely to be in the dead
of winter. One Christmas eve, when McAllen was
the hot spot in the nation at 92 degrees, we abandoned our carols and hot chocolate around the holiday tree, put on our swimsuits and went for a dip.

Maybe the vicious maligning originates in the
statistics. We are talking a whopping 312 days of
sunshine per year in the Rio Grande Valley. Of those
days, 117 days are 90 degrees Fahrenheit or above.
San Antonio averages slightly fewer, at 111 days;
Austin has 104 days at 90 degrees or above, and
Houston averages 92 days. The thing is, some of
these places and many others, like Dallas and Ft.
Worth, climb on up to 110 degrees and sit there day
after hellish day in the summer. Such a dastardly
thing doesn't occur very often in the Valley.

Of course, if you're playing golf, you probably
want one of those 312 sunshiny Valley days. You
notice it is hot when you play 18 holes of golf on
one of our 21 golf courses. And yes, there are vast

gardens to be tended, swimming pool waters to be stirred, *pachangas* where the social mores of swilling beer and devouring fajitas under mesquite trees must be scrupulously observed. If you think about it, there's a principle here: these activities are OUTDOORS and it's going to be warmer outdoors than INDOORS.

Maybe outsiders think the Valley is the Torrid Zone Capital because it takes them so long to get here and when they do, they're overdressed. Say they start out from San Antonio or Austin driving to the Valley for a convention or a wedding. They're wearing the clothes they wore to visit a castle in Germany: pussycat-bow polyester blouse and no-iron blend French-cuff shirt.

They drive a while and then they get scared. All they see is cactus and mesquite and hawks circling overhead, or are those things buzzards? The land is so flat they feel like they're driving in a trough. They look at the map and find they're only in Alice. Couple more hours oughta do it.

They arrive in McAllen about 3 p.m., when the sea breeze has pushed only as far as Weslaco. Folks are struggling up from under mesquites where they've been shooing fruit gnats and dozing off the Valley's famous "1015" onions they had for lunch. It's all too much. The visitors just *think* they're hot. Actually they're in metabolic meltdown from being overdressed and over-travelled.

We have a margarita waiting for these poor folks who feel that, the state map appearing gravitational, they have fallen hopelessly into the posterior exit of some cruel giant. We help them out of their civvies and into muu-muus and *guayaberas,* put them under a ceiling fan on a porch and tell them to move their lips slowly or not at all.

We tell them not to unpack their night creams and irons, because our lovely humidity naturally combats wrinkles of face and cloth. We tell them to quit fussing with their hair—let it blow. We call attention to how their emphysema and eczema have instantly improved.

The U.S. Weather Service tells us that if the temperature is 92 degrees and the humidity is 60 percent, we're in the "Rapidly Decreasing Work Efficiency" range. And if the water in the air should rise on up to 90 percent, our government declares that "nearly everyone is uncomfortable" and we're hovering in the "Danger Zone of Heat Prostration."

These statistics are worth heeding. They tell us Valleyites we'd better forget any Puritan work-ethic-type ideas (which mostly petered out in the Great Westward Push anyhow) and, with something cool to drink, go sit on the patio and watch the grackles.

In the charming book *Following the Drum* (Univ. of Nebraska, 1984) Teresa Griffin Vielé, an army wife living with her husband at Ft. Ringgold near Rio Grande City in the 1850's, observed that in the Valley "the climate was very salubrious, and cholera almost unheard of."

So if you're into cholera prevention, settle down. Just don't write back up north spreading silly rumors that it's hotter'n hell down in the Valley. It's not. It's salubrious. Healthy too.

Palm Reading

I was in a hurry but I stopped anyway. Workers were planting a palm tree on the beautiful University of Texas-Pan American campus. No ordinary nursery stock, all 40 feet of it stretched on a flatbed truck, from its matted nest of roots to its small topknot of delicate fronds. Its trunk showed a stretch of rich nut-brown fiber where it had been stripped of old growth.

Palm trees can be transplanted successfully even when they are full grown. Experts in this exotic activity stress that the palm must not be shocked by a sudden drop when it is taken up from its old location. It needs to be sustained by a crane, lowered and raised gently so it doesn't break or lose its crown.

Recently, an eighty-year-old palm was successfully transplanted from the corner of 23rd and Nolana in McAllen to a new location on Expressway 83 between McAllen and Mission. How? Very carefully.

Why? It didn't fit the decor of a discount shoe store parking lot.

As this one on the campus of the university lay like a trussed animal, a boom truck nearby guarding it with hook and chain, the heavy-duty digger lowered and raised its voracious head in 50-pound bites. Next came a gush of water into the hole from outsized hosing. The digger operator shut down his metal dinosaur and transferred to the crane on the boom truck.

I was more excited than I knew and called to a friend cycling by, "Hey, you better stop and watch this."

Now another worker adjusted the chain to allow better leverage, backed away, and signaled the operator. Up the giant staggered, peering into the third floor window of a nearby classroom building. For an instant, the 40 feet of tough fiber meandered in free space, dipping, flexing, testing the physics of flying. In seconds the great knitting ball of roots sank noiselessly into the hole.

Next, a crucial decision: Would it be upright or angled? How much angled? I thought how the flick of a worker's hand signaling to a crane operator would determine the skyline for 50 years.

The boss drove up. Had he been watching from across campus? He motioned to the operator. Straight up. They'd plant a little one soon by its side at an angle.

It was all over in 30 minutes. Like someone returning to the cemetery after the grave is closed, I came back later to check on the palm. It was swaying calmly, giant benign self enduring past the indignities of the day. It hadn't shot anyone, voted, marched in a parade, played pro ball, or logged committee time. It hadn't even protested its move. A great silent *fact* standing there with its feet in the mud. It was Being, both verb and noun.

For a moment I wanted to be a palm tree, some-one who accepts her luck without dropping a frond, someone in conversation with birds, an air-ranger. Fantasies aside, I thought the next best thing must be co-existing with these beauties.

THE PURSUIT OF HAPPINESS

It was the summer of '71 and we were on the road in the Pursuit of Happiness. We had three little boys, the biggest rental truck available filled with Early Marriage furniture, $700 in cash, and a crazy idea: Get back to the Rio Grande Valley. My husband had spent his high school years in La Feria, a little town in the mid-Valley, and the Valley was in his blood. When we graduated from the University of Louisville, he brought me back for a year in Edinburg and six in Harlingen. Then we moved away, upstate, to get some more education, agreeing that we probably would never return to the Valley to live. Too remote. Too provincial. Thanks but no thanks.

But four years and two degrees later, we discovered we'd exchanged orchards for used car lots, palm trees for security lights, and "God, how'd-you-do-it?" sunsets for urban pall.

One night, amidst dossiers and phone calls, we

made a list, like Ben Franklin recommended, of what we wanted in a locale: green grass, friendly folk—but not too many, moderate climate, clean air, a good school system, things to do. Oh yes, and space.

"Do you know where this is?" we sheepishly asked ourselves. So this was how we came to be caravaning to the Valley, looking like the Joads from the *Grapes of Wrath,* convinced we could eventually make a living for ourselves in our music and writing professions if we zeroed in on the right environment.

Once here, we began a tour of the countryside between McAllen and Edinburg looking for a farmhouse someone wanted to let us live in, preferably for nothing. With all our worldly goods simmering in the parked rental truck, our little boys whining and fidgeting in the back seat of the car, and nothing more than blind faith, we systematically crisscrossed north to south from Highway 107 to a dirt road known as Nolana on the north outskirts of McAllen, and then east to west from McColl Road to Ware Road.

The third day, we found a painter sprucing up an old farm dwelling on Minnesota Road. As the boys headed for the nearest irrigation standpipe, we learned that the owners, who lived up north, were planning to rent the place. We declared ourselves prospects and took the tour. The room called the bathroom housed only an old freestanding tub. The room known as the kitchen could be recognized by a hole in the wall where the sink pipe had once been. In the hallway, a little girl named Irma had immortalized herself with a signed self-portrait. The place would need a lot of work.

But outside, the boys had already begun a game of hide-and-seek in the forty acres of orange groves. So what could we do?

We got the owners' number and a few days later moved in, having reached an agreement that we would renovate the interior in exchange for several months' rent.

That next week, the older boys went to school at Jackson Elementary. But it rained that first day of September, as it did every other day that month in 1971, and so we had to drive them east on Minnesota, south on McColl, and back west on La Vista. The corner of Nolana and 2nd was a huge impassable pond.

Somehow we got through that year. We figured out how to get water from the canal, and then how to purify it enough to take a bath in it. We memorized the schedule of the ditch-rider, for he was the one who determined when we washed our clothes and filled our reservoir. We installed a kitchen sink and a bathroom toilet. Then we sanded floors and panelled walls (Goodbye, Saint Irma of the hallway). When a norther blew in, we noticed that we didn't have any means to heat the house, so we had to talk our landlords into installing a butane system.

We killed rats by the dozen and roaches by the hundred. We routed possums from beneath the house and challenged raccoons in the attic. Were we having fun yet? Was this the Pursuit of Happiness?

Meanwhile, our little boys made friends with an old guinea hen roosting in the orchard. "Coquena" shared the orchard with a remarkably shy English

sheep dog who darted in and out among the waxy leaves of the orange trees and thus earned the name of "Creep."

The boys rode the palm trees in our front yard that had been felled by some past hurricane and had partially uprighted themselves. They chased wild parrots and ate oranges, or tangerines, the tree of which, one son tells me now, they located by counting three rows over from the house and six back from the road.

They had a fondness for wading in a deep ditch by the standpipe, developed a loving friendship with a pony pastured at the corner of 2nd and Minnesota, and kept track of a nest of quail in a nearby field. And one son filled his entire lunchbox with baby frogs one afternoon on the walk from the bus stop.

That year we gleaned vegetables from already-harvested fields and from right-of-way spills. We picked carrots, by permission, from a field behind the orchard and grew greens in a garden. Every morning we drank ten-minute-old orange juice. We ate dates from the palms and enjoyed mulberry pie courtesy of an ancient tree on our lot.

In addition to these measures, we kept our bills paid by substitute teaching in school districts all around. For a long time afterward, my husband was greeted with "Hi, Coachie!" from little boys on the street.

Meanwhile, we had all made "town" friends, and, when spring came around, we began to have a virtual parade of folk, walking, cycling, or driving out from town on Saturdays and Sundays. They'd stand in the yard and call softly until one of us noticed them. Assured of our welcome, the adults flopped in the grass under the mesquites with coffee or water while the kids took off with ours to the orchard. Yes, we were having fun yet.

The Fourth of July. People asked shyly what we "might" be doing that day. They "might" come out. We decided to get organized. We'd cook the meat if everyone else brought a dish. So, on our spidery, rickety screened-in porch a table was laid fit for the gods. Amid the few patriotic trappings we could scour up as decorations, our friends placed deviled eggs and potato salad and beans and homemade bread and sliced garden tomatoes and brownies and coconut cake. And at dusk, in the old burr-ridden uneven yard, we set out our lawn chairs, flapped down quilts for the kids, and ate homemade mango ice cream, watching across the groves as fireworks whooshed up from McAllen.

Not too long after that, the place was sold and we were forced to move and buy a house in town. The boys pled with their dad to take the treehouse "in." No, boys, there are rules in town. Creep must be left behind, for an orchard dog would never be happy in town. And now we had to buy our oranges at the roadside stand like everyone else.

Even yet we dream of that little Eden. In one of my dreams, the house becomes available again and we move back. We occasionally still declare periods of mourning where we opine that we were not allowed to stay on, reveling in the locale, building on our initial hard-won efforts.

Where the forty acres of orange trees grew, a subdivision bloomed, complete with underground

utilities. Minnesota Road was renamed a flower
street, Violet. But in an eerie architectural afterlife,
our old farmhouse lived on for several years,
encircled by fine brick homes with pools and fences
and recessed garbage cans.

Back toward town, a townhouse development
sits where the quail's nest was, and the pony's lovely
pasture is just a vacant lot reserved for maintenance
equipment and utilities installations. And of course
the corner of Nolana and 2nd is passable,
even speedable.

Along with dreaming of it, we often laugh at
ourselves for sentimentalizing a place so hopelessly
old and rundown, and remember how backbreaking
the work was to redeem it from decrepitude. We
marvel that we had the nerve, the energy to attempt
something so preposterous. We would never begin
such a thing now, but the experience gave us, as our
grandmothers would say, starch.

In a paradoxical way, we're resentful that so
many people shared our common dream, to come to
the Valley and enjoy a good quality of life. So that
now we no longer have our Eden, even though, long
before the town grew north, we had become one of
the "town" visitors to that place ourselves.

But here is the point: we had the freedom to
become. We were allowed to choose, over and over
and over. To return to the Valley. To realize a
country-living fantasy. To educate our children in the
local schools. To seek our niche in the workplace.
Our best selves call us to grant that right to others
knowing that *preserving* the freedom must take
priority over *claiming* it.

Here in America we may rise and gather our children about us and strike out. With lightning swiftness, we re-pitch our tents, gamble our possessions, seek new friends, claim our priorities. All this with the backing of the Ninth Amendment, which says that we can do whatever we please unless it's expressly forbidden by law. In other words, Pursue Happiness.

In our family's pursuit, we long ago surrendered the old 30's farmhouse on Minnesota Road to "progress," our own and everyone else's. Still, it's fun to remember how we brought the stereo out to the creaky wooden porch that Fourth of July back in 1972 and had an afternoon of stirring Sousa marches, as loud as we wanted them, with hundreds of orange trees listening.

THE POSSIBLE POSSUM

I had seen her on occasion going over the wood fence of our city backyard, the large well-fed marsupial who had niftily raised a family under our hot tub. She seemed a fine subject for a photo, if we could only get her to pose. And we had added incentive to photograph a native creature on our premises. Our son Ansen had entered a local wildlife photography competition; my husband and I were signed up as the "landowners" on which the wildlife lived.

The night of the proposed shoot, we baited one end of a string and positioned it in the compost corner, running the other end into the house and attaching a small bell to it. Thinking we might be lucky to be roused by midnight, we settled in. With our photo equipment barely prepared, the bell rang loudly.

We raced to the compost corner. There she was, insouciant, possibly puzzled at why this chicken tidbit on a string was not behaving like fast food.

Crouched there in her luxuriant coat, she seemed even larger than I remembered her earlier, maybe six or seven pounds, a truly glorious specimen. My apple and potato peelings had done their job.

At her leisure she hid in the bougainvillea a few moments, then rose to the occasion by skinning the fence and perching there, obliging us with several seconds of studied hesitation that produced a winning photo in the nocturnal division of the Valley Land Fund contest.

Not long after that, we went on a little trip. When we returned, one of our neighbors reported he had picked up a board and soundly clobbered a large possum on our fence.

"Did you kill it?" I asked, unwilling to give him the bad news that he had possibly smashed an Oscar-winning possum.

"It left," he said. "By the time I got around to the other side, it was gone."

I breathed easier, and yet . . .we never saw our possum again.

Although people categorize this sometimes-city-dweller right up there with rats, grackles and snakes, this particular possum never bothered us, didn't eat our papayas or cause our non-existent dog to bark.

Oh, it lurked, maybe thumped. It had a bald ratty tail and a look in its eye of a different intelligence. And it had the nerve to play possum. That was about it. We had this funny notion that we could have cohabited peacefully with it, along with the geckos and anoles and kiskadee flycatchers and mesquites that claim Blk. 2, Thomas Terrace, City of

McAllen as their home too.

On awards night, I heard someone studying the program say, "The Seales? I didn't know they had a ranch!"

 SAFE

We are in what we call the Sunday evening hara-kiris. Except we say harrie-carries, the way we said it as children. My husband sulks over the week's lesson plans. Our son is made melancholy by the world situation reported in the Sunday paper. I am fuming about Monday's inevitable tasks. Then the phone rings: Will we come to the *palapa?*

Yes, of course. I finish the sandwiches I'm making and stash them in the fridge for Monday noon, grab the mosquito spray, and we three head north on the highway in November's early dusk.

The two little roadside communities play out, and we turn back west, passing flat farms and fields. We watch for a flag on a post and nose the Plymouth through an open gate, entering a world of tightly embraced cactus and mesquite.

This land has never been cleared. The island of natural brush in a sea of cultivated fields is a holdout for the owner, our friend Al who lives in town.

Al's family has been in *La Frontera* north of the
Rio Grande for eight generations. He bought the 16
acres, which he dubbed "*La Migaja*," the crumb, to
answer a need to reclaim his heritage. Its location is
traceable to one of the huge Spanish land grants
given to one of the families whom Al is undoubtedly
descended from. Al is hoping a son and the son's
son won't sell it to an orchard developer or
a rancher.

It is dark in here, darker than a closet. Now the
inkiness gives way to a little clearing and there is Al
readying the fire. We thread our way along a short
path to his newly renovated palapa.

Palapa. Palapa. The word tastes like exotic fruit,
makes the tongue indolent and naughty. This palapa
has been totally refurbished and it takes a while to
admire. A circular shelter built of native materials,
it's maybe 35 feet in diameter and sports a new
Saltillo tile floor.

The centerpole is an ebony trunk, as are the
smaller support poles around the edge, each chosen
for its sturdiness and correct height. Young willow
trunks connect the outer rim with the apex at the
centerpole. Strapped crosswise on the willows,
forming a circular pattern, is fresh bamboo, and
woven on to the bamboo, to make the thick roof, are
new cattail rushes.

The three who did the renovation have slipped
back into Mexico. Nothing much changes in this
structural form: it's cross-cultural, archetypal. We
laugh that this one has been fitted with an electrical
outlet.

Now Al's other guests arrive, among them a

couple from Washington, D.C. Don has spent a
lifetime of work in industrial health and safety. It
isn't long before Don reminds us that if we insist on
sitting leeward, someone's hair may catch fire from
the sparks of the mesquite burning briskly now in
the huge iron caldron. More to humor Don than to
take care, we move our chairs back a little.

Now we look up through the branches to see
the stars. Each is magnified by carats compared to its
city backyard version. In the distance through the
undergrowth, a cow bawls, a coyote howls.

When the food is ready, we repair to the palapa.
Al plugs in the overhead light to help the glow from
the citronella bucket flames and we settle in to, of all
things, bowls of ceviche prepared by our visitors
from the north. When the bowls are slurped clean,
they are returned to be refilled with soupy black
beans topped with dollops of rice.

Tortillas warmed near the open fire come
around. Everyone spoons and sops until groans of
satisfaction replace the silence of hungry folk eating
outdoors.

At ten a tiny TV is brought from a van. Seems
there's a local news story of particular interest to Al.
Our circular seating tilts.

"Good thing this palapa is not a boat!"

"Isn't this ridiculous, watching TV in an old
mesquite thicket?"

But the Sunday night movie is running overtime.
So a cellular phone is produced and a call made to
the station to see exactly how late the news feature
will be.

We agree we'll have time to get home before it's

broadcast. So why do we sit, linger on? No one is willing to break the spell. Then a peculiar sound emerges from the brush a few feet away.

"Listen!" someone says.

"What is that?"

"A pump."

"A car on the road."

"A motor of some kind."

Finally comes the definitive answer. "That's a rattlesnake."

No one moves. We listen to the ancient sizzle. The sound effervesces, is oddly steadying.

Then someone wants to see it. The flashlight illumines only a giant cactus—how old?—sitting like a stalagmite in the cave of the thicket.

The snake is finally quiet. We agree it was disturbed by something—surely not us—and has gone its way. Suddenly we laugh, are noisy on purpose. Everyone pitches in, and the palapa and clearing are clean in minutes. Still, we go more carefully along the path, and never without the light.

The fire is smothered and we climb into our cars and thread back to the road, back to town.

When we wake in the night, we know we have been dreaming of bigger stars. The pattern of the palapa roof wheels onstage. Our hair smells of mesquite smoke. From the mind's store comes the snake's song.

So much for harry-carry this week.

HOMETOWN

Hometown. It has two stressed syllables. It won't come out right if you try to hurry it.

Time was, your place of birth was your place of residence. Now life's not so simple. So your hometown can be either your birthplace, the place of your childhood, the town where you graduated from high school, or your present zip code.

I name at least two places my hometown. It's comforting to be able to switch, depending on the mood and the company I'm in. If I want to be counted as coming from the heart of Texas, the bedrock of all things ethnically Texan and thus presently chic, I say I'm from Waxahachie, population 17,600, central Texas. Waxahachie's the one with the fairy tale courthouse, a pink granite medieval castle plopped down in a cotton patch.

Otherwise, my hometown is McAllen, down in the Rio Grande Valley. As a citizen of McAllen for 23 years, and by careful choice, I'll defend my hometown against all comers. More on that later.

But first Waxahachie. For years after I graduated from Waxahachie High School, I avoided mentioning the name. I'd say I was from "near Dallas."
I wasn't exactly ashamed; it just wasn't the *thing* to be from a gently declining little town in Texas, a municipal rip Van Winkle.

Even more importantly, the name itself produced derisive laughter and ridicule: "Walksa-WHO?-chie," "Wacky-hacky?" "Did you say Nacogdoches?" There are lots of bad jokes, set in Waxahachie, about traveling salesmen or little old ladies. I've tried to figure out why, since the jokes don't seem to have a regional flavor. Maybe the locale was set in Waxahachie to give the kiss of outlandishness to the story, to put the story in such a crazy-named place that it was rendered harmless. After all, it *did* occur in that really unbelievable town called Waxahachie.

And then a funny thing happened: my provincial central Texas burg became famous. First, it was the Gingerbread Trail. In the shadow of the glass and chrome towers of Dallas and Ft. Worth, Metroplex glitterati came for an annual tour of the quaint fin-de-siècle homes which I as a child thought everyone in the world lived in. They stayed on to buy Depression glass and Tiffany windows and gingham bunnies and yellowed tatting in the town's antique shops.

And it didn't stop with the annual pilgrimage. Dallas professionals continue to snap up vintage two-story frame houses on Marvin Avenue and West Main Street at bargains of $300,000 for the privilege of replacing rotting L-shaped porches and installing bevelled-edge glass door panes.

Then there's the movie industry. Nearly 30 years ago, hometown favorite son Robert Benton returned to "Waxa" to film *Bonnie and Clyde*. That filming unleashed a flood from Hollywood on my pretty little town. To date, there have been over 40 other movies starring Waxahachie as location. In recent years, three movies made in Waxahachie have won major Academy Awards—*Tender Mercies, Places in the Heart,* and *The Trip to Bountiful.*

Your favorite hang-out was Kroger's, Sally Field? Puuullease! Why not Sims Library, built in 1904, or the Masonic Lodge, or the Chautauqua Auditorium in the park?

And the beat goes on. Some time back, my folks (you heard me: *folks*), who are retired there, took me for a drive one lazy afternoon. A point of interest was the back of the Presbyterian church "where Meryl Streep did a scene just last week."

The other recent fame, which threatened to over-shadow the Hansel and Gretel atmosphere and the moviemaking, had its own cast of thousands. Waxahachie was in the news as the epicenter of the futuristic superconducting super collider. Now, after several years of exciting the townfolk, dislocating families, and turning farms into installations, Congress has returned the remnants of Waxahachie to itself.

So Waxahachie's *one* of my hometowns. I'm a "Waxahachie Woman," just like the song says. When it's advantageous to use that identity, I do.

The other half of the time I claim to be from McAllen. Now there's a certain way upcountry people pronounce McAllen that lets you know they're about to ask if we have running water and indoor toilets. It makes the hair on my neck stand up. "Sooooo? You're from *MACK* Allen, are you?" All you who call McAllen hometown, check the nape of your neck. See what I mean?

Jim Stowell, who grew up on Seventh Street in McAllen, has written a book *Traveling Light* (Milkweed Editions, 1988) which details his zigzags across our country for 20 years. Jim doesn't live in McAllen anymore, hasn't for a long time. It's surprising therefore how much he mentions McAllen in the book. Or maybe it isn't.

Wherever Stowell is, hiding from a crazy behind a stack of tires in Idaho, locked up in the cell block at an air base for being AWOL, on a Greyhound to Tucson, he thinks and rethinks his relationship to the town he claims as home.

Mulling over a decision he must make, he writes, "Hell, I thought, when I left the Rio Grande Valley I was glad to leave it behind. Those people don't have anything to do with my life anymore. I don't have any past. What those people thought was cool or right doesn't make any difference to me any more." And yet, he made the conservative decision most of his old neighbors in McAllen would have made.

Another time, having been dropped off as a hitchhiker in the Rocky Mountains, Stowell asks himself, "What would those bozos back in the Rio Grande Valley say if they heard you'd been to the World's Fair?. . .Who would have ever thought back in the Rio Grande Valley, back in McAllen, Texas, that you would ever be here? Yeah, it's a lot different in the mountains than it is down in the valley. For one thing, it is cold as hell up here."

Stowell just can't get McAllen out of his mind, regardless of what it was or wasn't to him as a child. "Hell, half the streets in town weren't even paved until I was thirteen years old." One's hometown may be a genetic hallmark, a kind of imprint one carries throughout life.

In Waxahachie, the roots of cottonwood and oak, pecan and pyracantha have a habit of interrupting the sidewalks. Many a night I have drifted to sleep on the hop-whir-skip rhythm of my skates from that day's repetitions up and down the block. What is there so comforting about mastering the cracks in one's own sidewalk?

When I was growing up in Waxahachie we were mightily concerned with how Sandra Watman's children acted in the A&P on Tuesday morning. There was tremendous interest in a rumor that my geography teacher had been a lady wrestler at one time. And did the Methodists intentionally put their revival back to back with the Baptists'?

To grow up in Waxahachie or McAllen is to examine the cracks in the sidewalk, even to dream them. Lives take on a peculiar magnification of the ordinary in small towns. Stiflingly provincial, some would say.

Yet small-town life conforms curiously to Camus' definition of existentialism: real worth of life depends in large measure on the value placed on life by the one living it. We *thought* Waxahachie was our oyster, and so it was.

Now McAllen is my oyster. Let others say
MACK Allen; still, it's a good enough place to live,
and a whole lot better than most. Both by our local
efforts, and by default, the rest of the world is not as
alluring as it once was.

Yes, we have some knotty problems: auto theft,
house pillage, drug traffic, urban sprawl, seasonal
overcrowding, water quality—add your own to the
list. But have you noticed our healthy crop of young
adults? Funny, how a lot of them have the same last
name as folks who have been here a generation or
longer. Our kids are coming back—after the university scene, after a year or two in a big-city fast track,
after touring the world in uniform. Maybe, just
maybe, we're growing a batch of people that name
McAllen as their *only* hometown.

The world we McAllenites have chosen today is
here, in an adolescent city along the U.S. border,
where we have our own crazy mix of the harsh and
heavenly.

NAFTA is producing chain stores and superhigh-
ways and international bridges and export
houses in our area faster than we can count them.
We may lose the desirable aspects of provincialism,
the treasures of a hometown, in the stampede of
international trade.

So let the rest of the world be forewarned: we
are inhabitants. You know, like the snail darter and
the spotted owl. This is our *home*town, not just a
weighing station, an entryway, a truckers' route
between the U.S. and Mexico. This is our habitat.
We have wildlife rights.

All together now:
Hommmmmetownnnn....
    Nice sound, huh? It brims with memory,
identity, hope. Take comfort in it. Hang on to it.

Garlic and Other Children

Alexander Pope probably wasn't learning any Spanish when he wrote, "A little learning is a dang'rous thing." Or if he was, he had only learned the word for eye, *ojo*, by then, and had mistaken bliss for ignorance.

He hadn't learned that garlic was *ajo*, that leaf was *hoja*, that daughter was *hija*, and son was *hijo*. No wonder he had time to sit around composing couplets.

There was a time when I was very happy with my little Spanish. I would ask people how their *ojos* were if I noticed they had been *rojos*. I would also be careful not to put the *mal de ojo* unwittingly on some sweet baby in the grocery store by admiring it too strongly with my greenish eyes. My little knowledge was anything but dang'rous.

Enter the day I was preparing a dish using garlic. Fool that I was, I asked a friend nearby its name in Spanish.

"*Ajo*," she answered.

"Ah-hah!" I said.

"No, *ajo*," she corrected.

"Oh yes, I understood," I reassured her. "I had just thought of a way to remember it: Don't get *ajo* in your *ojo*."

She smiled, forgiving my need for a mnemonic device for anything that simple. And my little learning continued to be an innocuous thing.

But one day in early spring someone directed my *ojos* to the *hojas* on the trees. I looked vainly for cloves of garlic miraculously growing twelve feet up. Then I realized that wasn't my word. And standing there like a latter-day Eve staring up at the leaves, I lost my linguistic innocence. Two words were company; three, a crowd.

The tale is nearly finished. All that remains to be said is that the day arrived when I learned people had relatives called *hijas* and *hijos.*

Alexander Pope, you are not my friend. Your pronouncement of the dangers of skimpy knowledge is in itself a dang'rous thing.

I learned too much. Now I am World Champion of the Conversational Pause. Listen to me:

"Mrs. Hinojosa, how are your—(seconds tick by. . . I am sorting frantically through the eyes and leaves trying to find the sons and daughters). . . *ajos?*"

Mrs. Hinojosa looks at me kindly. "My garlic is just fine," she says in perfect English. "How is *your* garlic?"

So, Mr. Pope, go back to your stuffy eighteenth century and take your adage with you. I find greater comfort in the words of your ancient philosophical predecessor Festus: "Much learning doth make thee mad."

How Soon Is The Fig Tree Withered Away!

MATTHEW 21:20

T his morning when my husband and I walked by the place where the old hotel had stood, the ghosts of old whores whispered to us.

In the western sky a smattering of stars enclosed a waning moon. In the east, the sky was paling to blue with streaks of pink heralding the sun climbing up out of the Gulf. A host of pigeons rose from the tall palms facing the construction site and crossed over the gleaming, fresh-poured cement to a row of old palms in the next block.

They could have lit in our fig tree, had it been there. What is there in its place, as far as I can tell from the times I have walked over there and stood watching the workmen, is a vent for a toilet.

Once the lot was the site of the hotel where relatives stayed when they came into town for a wedding or funeral. It sat on a whole prime city block surrounded by palm trees filled with parrots and pigeons and dates. Over the years the building dwindled to a fire-prone haunt for drug dealings and quick sex, a roach-infested flim-flam of an edifice. Even the sentimental agreed that the structure had seen a better day.

Three years ago, when the wrecking crew came and for days hauled away the old landmark building, the neighborhood was abuzz with possibilities for what might replace it. Some entertained the rumor that because there were still so many trees and shrubs, (and for whatever reason, the crew had been careful not to harm them) the block was going to be made into a city park. In fact, when the old walls came down, an entire tropical garden was disclosed in the private courtyard where the pool had been.

Among the giant schiffleras and tall ragged banana plants, the fragrant gardenias and frangi-pangi, stood an old-fashioned fig tree. It and the palm trees soon became the sole inhabitants of the block, the more fragile plants quickly dying without the protection of the old structure.

Fig trees have an honored and holy provenance. They flourish and wither throughout the Bible, the absence, ripeness or rottenness of their fruit assigned moral value. The prophet Jeremiah preached about bad figs, which he proclaimed "naughty," "vile," and "evil", and good figs, graded "first ripe" or "very good." Fig leaves, sewn together, provided the first antidote for shame for Adam and Eve.

Our fig tree was of good moral character, for it apparently had kept bearing year after year, despite not being pruned or fertilized, despite the Johnson grass that grew waist-high around it and the traffic fumes which drifted over it and the vandals who broke off its limbs and carved its trunk.

The day we discovered it had ripe fruit, we thrashed around on the lot until we located an old plastic bag and proceeded to fill it with Jeremianic "first ripe" figs.

After that, when we struck out in the pre-dawn, we took a bag to pick the day's figs, before the grackles and wasps found the ones that had blushed in the night from their hard green selves to tender iridescent orbs. Miraculously—and this raised the ante on our luck—no other human beings in the neighborhood seemed to care a fig about figs.

Sometimes, as we picked, the perfection of a certain fig we ran across overcame us and we would celebrate our luck and the goodness of the tree by showing it to the other, then, on site, pop it into our mouth, coming down on the incredible sweetness made up of the hundreds of minute interior flowers that give the fruit its unique masticatory essence.

In June of the third year of our love affair with the fig tree, we came upon a tank truck backed into the lot watering a cluster of new palms that had been planted the day before. The older palms—the ones that had towered thirty feet in the air and had survived a number of hurricanes and were always filled with birds and had been used in foregrounds of pictures with spectacular sunsets in chamber of commerce brochures—these had been trimmed and balled and taken up for relocation. For now, they lay about on the ground like mortal pharaohs without burial chambers.

Yet the fig tree still stood, and so we entertained hope against hope that it was not going to be taken.

Maybe we should have made placards of protest right then. Should have paraded on the edge of the street with our signs just as one lone ordinary woman had done across town recently on the day they took out a cluster of healthy landmark palms in the name of progress.

We didn't care if we never ate another fig from the tree. We didn't care if we couldn't see it, or get to it anymore. We just wanted it to live. It deserved life. We had begun to count it a talisman, a small prayer, a stay against the entropy of progress.

And so we waited. Each morning as we rounded the corner, we grew silent, strained to see it . . . and there it was. We convinced ourselves it was being incorporated into the new plans.

Another July came and we waded into the tall grass to check daily the ripening of another season's figs. We picked only the ripe ones and hauled them home, eating a few for breakfast, saving the rest until we had enough to cook with a little lemon peel and sugar and put in clean mayonnaise jars for the freezer.

After a few days, two ominous signs appeared on the lot. One, a literal sign in the form of a portable drag-in read:

COMING SOON TO THIS LOCATION
BUSINESS PLAZA
OFFICE SPACE AVAILABLE

The other sign was a bulldozer-wide strip of soil scraped of careless weeds and Johnson grass running the length of the lot.

Here was evidence of change, and yet nothing else happened. We held our breath and picked figs.

One morning, coming up the driveway with the day's figs in tow, we heard the phone ringing insistently. It was my 82-year-old mother upstate, who had been in bed a few days recovering from a mysterious fall. Now she sounded shaken and frightened. The EMS people had just taken Dad to the hospital. My sister, living in the same town, had been called away the day before. I showered and caught a plane.

The fig tree did not cross my mind until many mornings later. By now, my father had come home from the hospital, his heart settled down a while longer. My mother had begun practice walks slowly about the house with a cane—the original fall had either actually been or portended a slight stroke. I was getting anxious to go south again, where I knew my desk was piled high with mail, the garden overgrown, the birds thirsty.

We three were at table that morning having breakfast, one of the few times we'd managed a quorum for a meal. Suddenly Mother stopped her laborious chewing. "It's August," she said. "My fig tree. I nearly forgot."

She rose and went to the kitchen window. "It's ready." She bent to the cabinet, got a pan and started for the back door. Dad and I had to quit our cereal and go with her to steady her.

And from that day forth, Mother rose to supervise the harvest of the day's figs. We carried a chair out to the fig tree for her in the early morning light and then helped her, with her long robe and

stumbling houseshoes and teetery walker, to get to it.
There she instructed us as to ripe or unripe, big
enough or not, until we had picked the dozen or so
fruits that constituted that day's take.

Meanwhile, foil pans had to be tied to the
branches to scare away the birds. Dad insisted on
going up and down a stepladder to tie them strategi-
cally about though when he came down he was pale
and his hands trembled. He vowed that was enough
of *that* though it was obvious he was pleased to be
pleasing his wife.

There was a great deal of protocol, as there
always is in our mother's kitchen, to preparing the
figs. First we had to peel them, a seriously tedious
task, because Mother had evolved a theory that their
skins might be tough. A big kettle with a touch of
water, a careful cutting of the fruit into halves or
quarters, some lemon peel, sugar, then bringing all to
a gentle boil and stirring, stirring, stirring. The figs
were a big bother and I took their preparation as a
barely tolerated whim of my mother.

My sister is peculiarly not gifted in the very
things she hates to do, and, back in town again, she
declared herself not a gifted canner of figs. But even
she ended up canning a quart of the rosy knobs one
day when I was off on R&R.

For we both knew that the figs meant a great
deal to our mother and so we humored her. They
were one means by which she was regaining her will
to live, for she is a woman who lives to eat, and she
not only delighted in the taste of figs but claimed all
sorts of miraculous healing properties for them.

But what about our figs at home? By that time I

didn't care if I ever ate another fig. Still . . . still
there was the tree. The tree had survived, cheerfully,
had waited for us each summer. We were downright
fond of the tree. It too was a thing to get up for on
a sweltering Texas summer morning. I lay on my cot
in my father's study and wondered about *my* fig tree.
A mother's and daughter's love for their respective fig
trees was not lost on me; I smiled in the dark.

On the phone my husband hedged. "You can
see for yourself when you get home."

I was dead weight in the car coming home from
the airport. The struggle had lasted several weeks. I
had left my parents better, never well again, but
propped up for now, making do with the years that
had suddenly hurled themselves against their genteel
old age. Picking a few figs every morning. "Putting
them up." Strong genetic signals out of their agrarian
pasts. Their figs were much larger than ours, testimony to their care of the tree the rest of the year,
denial that there would ever come a summer when
no one would be there to cherish them.

I guess I knew that our fig tree was gone before
I saw the big empty hole of sky. When we rounded
the corner, there was nothing, nothing on the huge
lot except the tenuous new palm cluster, some con-
crete foundation forms and iron reinforcements, and
the flashing portable sign advertising office space.

"Forgive me, tree, I take you for good use,"
intones the *herbera* before harvesting a medicinal
plant. The same could not be spoken to our fig tree,
lying somewhere ignominiously with a hundred other
trees uprooted that day. Nor to the others like it

being sacrificed daily in our Rio Grande Valley as the North American Free Trade Agreement literally paves over the open fields, the orchards, the old neighborhoods, gouging out everything that was planted with care and love, that has sunk its roots in the rich alluvial soil over the decades, that has survived desert drought and hurricane winds and river flooding.

It is not the same: developers sodding little strips of St. Augustine along the curb, establishing a few blooming ornamentals around the order stations of fast-food installations, substituting three small nursery palms on a parking lot in place of a clump of eighty-year-old giants that served as home for a number of animals.

It's not the same: furnishing every tract house with a cute little three-foot junior oak, hoping the occupants of the new development will water it.

"The vine is dried up, and the fig tree languisheth; the pomegranate tree, the palm tree also, and the apple tree, even all the trees of the field are withered; because joy is withered away. . . ." (Joel 1:12)

Still, there's its cousin, my mother's fig tree a few hundred miles north, putting out—gratis and juicy, cheering life on in my tired old mother and father where joy is not quite withered away. Testimony of what is meant to be the deep, eternal connections between plants and animals.

Is it too late to honor the spirit of the generous and magical plant world? Will we be happy only when the last office building supplants the last fig tree? Don't we see the connection between a tree and joy?

"Now learn a parable of the fig tree."
(Mark. 13:28)

Getting It Together At Falcon

The time seems light years ago. We went, the same as you did, or do. On a last fling before school started. That year, ours was an overnight camp-out, just up the country at Falcon State Park where the Rio Grande is dammed one last time as it starts its flow to the Gulf.

We got the outing accident over before we even left home. The smallest boy walked into the oldest one's fish hook as they were packing the car. A major cry, a little bloody scratch, several kisses later we were on our way.

Our dachshund Taffy, dubbed the Brown Nuisance, kept our affections on a roller coaster. We hated her when she bounded out of the car, pawing a fresh scar on a boy's leg. We loved her when she kept on swimming, rhythmically, little front paws methodically pushing and pulling and tail rotating like a helicopter blade, even when we lifted her high out of the water. We hated her when she slipped her collar in the night and we had to go hunting for her. We loved her when she warned us of a snake ahead on the path.

My husband made an exquisite campfire stew from scratch. He served our plates at 9 p.m., went over and turned on the car lights briefly, hollered, "Everybody, take a good look at your stew!" then snapped us into stew-eating darkness. We had forgotten a light.

I woke up three or four times in the night, remembering there were stars out here away from city street corner wattages. I crawled out and gazed up at the shimmering, reeling, eternal ceiling and wondered how the speck-on-the-speck-meaning-me could possibly hope to understand what she was seeing.

The coyotes were crying, strong and willful, and I said thanks that there were still places one could hear wild things in the night.

The geometric lines of pink and blue in the pre-dawn sky caught the camp rabbits foraging around the garbage cans. The Brown Nuisance saw and grumbled but lay still, fascinated and outdone by the rabbits' audacity. A curve-billed thrasher came visiting for a stray corn chip.

We walked far down the shore. "Here it is!" exclaimed our eleven-year-old. "Here's my place, and I thought it was gone!" The gooey mud where we were walking changed to a watery desert of untouched rippled sand. "This is the best feeling in the whole wide world," he crooned as he watched his feet disappear in the silky shallows. He was eons from books and pencils.

High noon. Time to go back to camp.
No more Thursday noons on the water for a while.
"Watch that jagged shell!" I called to the little boy as
we filed up the path.

"Oh, how pretty!" He shamed me, picking it up
and placing it gently with the others in his soggy
towel.

Then it was time to go home. The boat-tailed
grackles jawed over the leftovers of the sandwiches.
Everyone was a little tired, a little sad at leaving, a
little mixed up about going home to school.

The boys looked toward the south at the gates of
the dam. "There's the whole dam thing," quipped
the junior high one with a twinkle in his eye that
said he was semantically insulated against
correction.

"Mother," spoke up middleman, dreamily
fingering an opalescent mussel shell, "if there is
mother-of-pearl, is there father-of-pearl too?"

I think about the rabbits, the coyotes, the grackles, the Seales. "Why not? It sounds right
to me."

ONE DAY IN THE LIFE OF A SOUTH TEXAS JUROR

At five minutes before nine on a Monday morning in December, I hurry toward the Hidalgo County Courthouse, a plain hulking sandstone building made huge by Edinburg's surrounding small shops and offices. I look up, surprised by a pale waning moon in the west gracing a cloudless azure sky. It's a poetic sight, incongruous with what I am about to do.

"*Perdón!*" I say, "*Perdón!*" as I push through the men lingering about the auditorium door smoking. It is nearly time and some grind their stubs on the sidewalk or flip them onto the grass. They follow me inside.

About 150 prospective jurors are sitting in the small auditorium. It could not be more hushed at the tomb of Father Hidalgo. Are the summoned scared or sleepy? It is hard to tell. Near the back, I pick my way over several people, a man immobilized by new high-topped boots, a woman reeking of

Estée Lauder, a teenager temporarily prevented from rising when the handle of his hip pocket comb catches on the seat. I ease down near a young woman idly zipping her purse open and shut, adding my own silence to the group.

I count them: this is the fourth time I've been called to jury duty in as many years. It's the second time this year, and when I phone earlier to explain that I've *been* on a jury, actually sat on a trial six months earlier, the third clerk I am referred to tells me I must appear anyway. "We cleared the jury wheel in July and started again. It doesn't matter if you served already."

So this is a cross-section of Hidalgo County voters. I am told that about a fourth of the 600 people who may be called on a Monday morning will actually show. The others claim exemptions or their cards get lost.

Most of my general jury panel colleagues fall into a 30-55 age group, bracketed by a smattering of elders and teens. I note the ethnic make-up: eight Anglos, one black man, the rest a firm Hispanic majority. Some of the women jiggle babies and toddlers. Several men sit like chieftains, their straw Stetsons or black felt hats planted firmly on their heads. This Texas machismo will soon be dealt with.

We sit on, moments of restiveness passing over the group sporadically in whispers, low chuckles. Everyone is clean; everyone is ready. We finger our cards, neurotically going over our answers:

"Well, I *haven't* ever been charged with a felony, have I?"

"Let's see . . . I cut my finger twenty years ago

and had two stitches—but is *that* sustaining acciden-
tal bodily injury requiring medical attention?"

"Is it 17, or 18 years I have lived in this county?"

My purse-zipping seatmate zips open her purse
for the hundredth time, produces a pen, and changes
"Catholic" to "Christian" under "Religion" on her card.
She studies it further. "Do you sign it down here?"
she whispers to me.

"Just if you qualify for exemption," I whisper
back.

At 9:20 a woman appears on the floor level in
front of the stage. She is the jury clerk, deputized by
the district clerk. The judge will be here in a while.
First, though, all those not reading or writing English
are to come forward.

"*Buenos dias*," she begins again, for those who
do not speak it either, and we hear her message
repeated in Spanish. She retires to a table at the side
and a line of fourteen presumably monolingual
people forms before her up one aisle. She takes a
moment with each, then they walk across in front of
everyone, with slow, deliberate step or quick, hurried
gait, and disappear out a side door—forever, for all
the rest of us know. So goes a man with a colorful
kerchief around his neck, a woman cocooned in a
bright, striped *rebozo,* a young man with white
patches from a fresh shaving of his sideburns.
Actually, there go some of the more interesting-
looking people in this crowd.

"Hear ye! Hear ye! All rise!" the judge's bailiff
calls from the edge of the stage. She's an unlikely
looking bailiff, I'd say 22, silently asking us not to
hate her for her wanton mass of brown hair. As the

judge enters, we struggle up, stiff from the long sit.
Just as we're about to get our clothes straightened,
our hands respectably behind us, he bids us
be seated.

I settle back for the pep talk. One judge whom I
drew twice before had a celebrated habit of talking
more than an hour to prospective jurors. He started
back with World War II, ranged through the Vietnam
War, Watergate, the Supreme Court, our democratic
system, the NFL, his number of years on the bench,
his grandchildren, what his wife said at breakfast,
how we were not to assume we'd been kept waiting
because he was late—he wasn't: he was doing
mightier works in his chamber, and please do not
chew gum or say hello to any lawyer in the hall, I
don't care if he's your child's godfather or your next
door neighbor or your hunting buddy or your
cuñado, and this is America, not some foreign
country with repressive police systems and
kangaroo courts.

Now this judge admonishes us—thank God with
more brevity if not so entertainingly as the other—
and at the end of fifteen minutes, for a little stretch,
we are allowed to rise and take the oath, to do our
work to our best and so forth, but at the end we
can't determine whether to say "I will" or "I do" so it
comes out a pathetic murmur across the room.

We are seated again and the judge leads us
through all the exemptions. He says several times
that certain people may be "exempted to serve" and
we presume he means exempted *from* serving.
Whatever. When it comes to those over 65, he tells
them that they may serve if they feel they are

"hale and hearty," for "old age is wisdom, and wisdom is welcome in this court."

As for family excuses, anyone with an old mother, a *viejita* at home that is bedridden, "well, that's certainly an excuse." Only in the Valley.

As we come to the judge's light-hearted explanation of how the felons among us may slither to his chamber during recess, and how those of us with unsound mind or character may determine our own lack of fitness to serve, laughter explodes in palpable relief from the enforced silence of the last hour. There's a general shifting like a giant wave across the crowd, a sudden epidemic crossing and uncrossing of legs and arms.

Meanwhile, the district clerk in ankle-length hot pink pleated knit suit and pink lizard heels steps up her surveillance of us. She has been prowling the aisles for the last fifteen minutes, her movement contrasting our stillness. She orders the goat-ropers and other macho wonders to remove their top gear. At one point she tells a man to stop reading his paper. She seems to be counting us over and over. When the judge pauses to introduce her, she waves a pretty hand at us and beams as though she were seeing us for the first time.

While he's at it, the judge introduces his other help by name—the jury clerk, the assistant jury clerk, his bailiff—all women. "These fine ladies do all the work around here," he says, and the men in the crowd cackle and snort.

We are released at 10:15 for the judge to hear excuses. About thirty women queue up outside the women's restroom. My bladder is a veteran juror:

I know a second floor restroom. As I climb the wide polished stairs, I recall an incident from the last time I served. From the courtroom we heard running, shouts, a banging door, whoops and hollers. Later we learned from our judge that a defendant had made a break from another courtroom and been tackled on this landing. He admonished us weary jurors, only half-jokingly, not to follow suit.

Back in the auditorium now, the clerk tells us it will be a little while before our names come down on lists for the various assigned panels. My seat partner and I talk, and finally, running out of anything to say, we share my newspaper.

A young woman in jeans and athletic jacket slides in behind us. "Hey, Lucy," she whispers, recognizing the woman beside me. "What have I missed? I forgot and went to work and my boss reminded me. I had to drive like crazy from Harlingen."

Now the first group of names is called, with the prospective jurors coming forward to sit in order on the first three rows. It seems inordinately hard to get people to sit in the right order. The clerk points and cajoles, taps her foot, studies her list, chews her gum. I become so bored (or is it tense?) waiting for my name that I begin fantasizing which names I'd rather have been christened. "Valentina" is my first choice, with "Abelarda" and "Juventina" runners-up. The woman beside me starts at every "Maria." Seven Maria Somethings go by before she hears her special compound, Maria Lucila.

Another recess and we mill about, eyeing each other like passengers on a doomed plane. It's 11:00

a.m. now and we're reassembled for another group
to be called out, seated in order—with difficulty—
and led off. Thirty-five of us survive this cut. We are
told to hang around. A feeling out of childhood
grows on me and it's a little while before I can
identify it: the dread shame of being chosen last,
by default, for the softball team at recess.

The clerk returns at 11:30 to tell us to report
back at 1:30. Women form shopping teams and men
look around, inquiring pitifully where's a good place
to eat. It's been a while since I've had any of the
Echo Hotel's *envueltos,* soft tortillas filled with chick-
en and avocadoes and crowned with lettuce and sour
cream. I head in that direction for a solitary lunch
and a cruise through Wal-Mart.

Moving as in a dream, we reassemble at 1:30,
smelling of garlic and onions and cumin, leaden-eyed
and longing for the medically necessary siesta.
(Today, though it's December, the temperature is 93
degrees, the humidity at 69%.)

When the clerk calls "Juan Seale," I rise and go
forward. Jan? Juan? That's close enough:
I'm getting more flexible.

Maintaining our seating order, we are led upstairs
to a small district courtroom. The lawyers are
already squared off and they immediately begin to
look us over and whisper to their assistants as they
identify those of us they know. The judge is on the
bench. We are told this is a case concerning workers' compensation. We are about to be examined for
fitness to serve on a jury. We are not to take the
questions asked of us personally. Then the lawyer
for the injured party begins.

First he asks for a show of hands of those who have ever watched *Perry Mason* or *L.A. Law*. He tells us this is a civil case, that no one has done anything wrong. He tells us who he is, where his law office is located, and how many years his firm has been in practice. By the way, he's 42. He points to a couple of women perched in the jury box and says these young ladies will be assisting him with this *voir dire*, emphasizing the term but never defining it. (I wonder how many people know the term. I certainly wouldn't know—it's the examination of prospective jurors—had I not by this time had a career in jury service.)

He explains the case to us. A woman claims permanent disability from an injury on the job. She needs an expensive operation. Does she need it because of the injury, or from a pre-existing condition? The insurance company says she was born this way. The lawyer tells us the name of the local company employing her. Oh yes, it has changed its name. What, he asks the court reporter, is the name that was the "subsequent predecessor"?

I'm still chewing on that when he begins to identify us by name, ask occupations. Yes, she's a teacher at Seguin Elementary in McAllen. He's an assistant principal in Pharr. She's a housewife in Donna. He works in agriculture.

This man worked in an iron forge plant for 32 years. He has a hearing loss. And how does he feel about workers' compensation?

Would the lawyer repeat the question, please?

Oh yes, he's retired but he wishes he had had workers' compensation.

"If you're chosen for a jury, can you hear in this courtroom?"

"If you don't whisper," says the man.

We move on with the *voir dire*. The lawyer calls the names of two people he knows as teachers in a little upper Valley town notorious for its isolationism and nepotism. "Now, you two are out there in the pits," he begins. He knows one is the supervisor of the other. If they were both selected for the jury, would the underling let the supervisor tell him how to vote?

"No," says the mere teacher, looking back anxiously at his supervisor. "Sometimes things come up and he wants it one way and I want it the other. We go"—and he pauses, frustrated, then demostrates with opposing fingers, "we go—*contra*." The lawyer is satisfied.

We stop and learn our lessons for the day, definitions provided on printed posters. What is WORKERS' COMPENSATION? What is a PRODUCING CAUSE? What is an INJURY? What is TOTAL DISABILITY?

The young man beside me, identified at 19 as the youngest on the panel, jiggles his leg rapidly, vibrating the bench on which eight of us sit. He works in produce at a local grocery store. He asks me in a whisper if I want to be chosen. "Sure," I whisper back.

"I hope I'm not," he says. "I've got too much to do."

Suddenly I am his mother and I am furious. Lettuce washer, indeed! The lawyer is telling a story about lying to his parents when he was a child.

I lean over and whisper to the young man, "You better hope you are. It's the best education you'll ever get." Out of my mouth, it sounds preachy, but I'm not sorry I say it.

Now the lawyer is talking about his school-teaching experience. He couldn't make a living at it "'way back then, heh, heh." He realizes he's talking to five or six school teachers who have *not* become lawyers.

"Ms. Jan Seale," he reads from the cards, "isn't your husband—?" and he names my spouse's profession. Not sure what this has to do with my fitness as a juror, I reply in the affirmative. Everyone swivels and gawks.

It occurs to me I haven't given enough thought to what a public figure's wife is supposed to wear. Suddenly I'm aware that I have worn my black T-shirt with "City Lights Bookstore/ San Francisco" blazoned in silver on the front.

"Have you had any education whatsoever past high school?"

"Yes."

"Tell us where you went to school."

I tell him.

"It says here you're a writer, is that right?"

"Yes."

"What do you write?"

Actually I am fresh back from teaching at a poetry conference but I know better than to include poetry in the things I write. The mention of poetry will bring on a diatribe against the lawyer's English teacher for forced memorizations, or a line or two proudly declaimed from *Evangeline* or *Julius Caesar.*

So I say "articles and short stories."

"How do you feel about workers' compensation?" He has already asked at least fifteen prospective jurors. We've got it down to "I'm for it," and "It's a good thing." It's right up here with motherhood and tortillas on our favorite things list.

I decide to give a little variation. "I believe it's a reasonable solution for injured workers in a democratic society."

The judge is suddenly awake. "What number is that juror?" he bellows. I've said "democratic" and he heard it with a capital "D." He wants to put me on the telephone committee for his next election campaign.

We've been here an hour and fifteen minutes. We've gone over the "producing cause of injury" definition until we can say it in our sleep. We know we must vote as we find the "preponderance of evidence"—not as we feel. The other lawyer, obviously a foreigner from Houston, asks us if we can "set up 'ere" in the jury box and be fair and impartial. He illustrates personal bias by telling us a story of a bet he made with a buddy from Texas that Oklahoma would win the annual Texas-O.U. game. Oklahoma was skunked, and he knew they would be, and he had to buy a steak dinner. He did not place his bet on the "pre*pon*derance of evidence" nor was he "fair and impartial." He placed it on his loyalty. Did we understand the difference? The wooden seats are becoming very hard.

We take a break at 3:15, and when we are ushered back fifteen minutes later, we find a case being heard in the courtroom, apparently that of a

man accused of running a betting operation. The
man's five-year-old daughter sits in a chair near the
railing. Oblivious to her father's plight, she holds her
long brown hair crisscrossed over her head, forming
two large rabbit ears. The judge asks if this is the
man's daughter and why she is in the courtroom.

"Your honor, we didn't bring this child in the
courtroom to get sympathy from you. It's just that he
didn't have anyone to leave the child with," says the
defense lawyer. It seems the man's wife has died
recently.

The judge turns to other matters. "Why didn't
someone tell me earlier that this man had honorably
served his country, huh?"

The state's lawyer answers, "Ordinarily we don't
bring up military records unless the accused has been
dishonorably discharged."

"Well, that's too bad," the judge says. "I like to
know if a man has served his country. It makes a
difference."

The man is given a probated sentence and a fine.
His lawyer asks the court to assure extra payment for
fees she incurred for investigating the charges. The
judge laughs and brings down the gavel.

Now we're back, seated higgledy-piggledy this
time, awaiting the outcome of our examination.
Susan, the only acquaintance I've recognized all day,
and I have spoken at the break and now we sit
together in pale, light-eyed suspense at the make-up
of the jury. There are two other Anglos on the
panel, both, we presume, disqualified for their
answers. There's an old joke that most juries in
South Texas must contain at least a token minority

person, that is, at least one Anglo. If so, I was the
token *gringa* in the jury I served on six months
earlier.

(My husband was the only Anglo once when he
served. Although he speaks Spanish, he had to ask
the fellow jurors to speak English when they began
their deliberations, for fear he would miss something
important. For this they immediately elected him
foreman, a curious South Texas justice.)

As Rodriguez, Jimenez, Garcia, Garza, etc. are
called to take their places, Susan and I sit like Miss
America finalists, wondering which will be picked.
The twelfth juror is called, Mr. Alvarez. It's not Susan
and it's not me. And it's not the boy lettuce washer.
Too bad. He'll have to learn his justice from
L.A. Law and *Night Court.*

We are thanked and dismissed, going in a jumble
of relief and disappointment. We walk out in the
dazzling South Texas sun. Some store on the square
is broadcasting tinny Christmas carols. The silver glitter wreaths strung across Business Highway 281 bob
gently in the Gulf breeze that regularly moves inland
late afternoon. Bank time is 4:32. Temperature:
down to 91.

I shade my eyes and survey my homeland. I
have done my civic duty one more time here in our
beloved Rio Grande Valley of Texas. I'm a kid
coming out of the Saturday afternoon movie, a little
dizzy at the change. Aw-shucks, real life again!

INLAND TERRITORY

Recognizing Freedom

Freedom. Maybe the word conjures up a liberty bell, a quill pen, a vacationing family, a head bowed in worship. On Independence Day I think of Uncle George, the Paul Bunyan of my mother's family. He paced out his democratic citizenship in giant strides. Uncle George was the epitome of something elusive we like to dub "the American character."

Born a hundred miles north of Amarillo in a white clapboard farmhouse set back from the bend in the road, George grew up thinking normal visibility was the seven miles north to the Canadian River. He had four sisters and three brothers, big rawboned people fit to work the land and be worked by it. But George had other ideas.

That great expanse of Panhandle sky bewitched him and he signed on for meteorological training at MIT after he finished basic training in the Navy. Aboard an aircraft carrier, he astutely forecast a huge storm in the Leyte Gulf near the Philippines and won a Navy commendation for battling the weather.

When he came back home to Texas after World
War II, as Lt. Commander Henderson, he was
through with regimens and uniforms. Civilization
had imposed itself rather presumptuously on Uncle
George. After all, he'd been stationed in New
Orleans and San Diego and Pensacola and the
Philippines and New Zealand, and that was quite
enough people, thank you, to last a lifetime. So he
bought himself thirteen acres of the Henderson
homestead tract, drilled 232 feet through the cap rock
for good water, and built a little white stucco house
and filling station. He started selling gasoline and
fixing anything on wheels that crippled up or was
hauled in from a fifty-mile radius.

Why didn't he farm, go in big with the rest of the
family? For him, truth was self-evident: "I've milked
too many cows already."

Growing up, I spent a big part of every summer
with Aunt Irene and Uncle George. And a big part
of each of those visits was keeping Uncle George
fed. At noon my aunt and two cousins and I
scurried from kitchen to dining room loading the
table with cornbread, blackeyed peas, chicken-fried
steak, mashed potatoes, fried okra, and fresh sliced
tomatoes from the garden.

I was often sent to fetch Uncle George when
dinner was "on." Bareheaded and barefoot in the
noonday sun, I skipped across the yard and through
sandy tire ruts to the gaping door of the shop. The
flying red horse sign squeaked a little in the breeze.
Smokie or Louie or Pucker—whatever good old dog
someone had given Uncle George—ambled along

behind. Three or four country philosophers stood about the door to catch the breeze and shoot it as well. I squinted in the cool dimness, looking for a pair of big greasy boots. Something moved and the dog went for it. I walked through the group of men, silent now because a young lady was present, and squatted beside a jacked-up truck. "Uncle George," I said, addressing the Size 12 boots, "dinner's ready."

"Thank the Lord," a voice said, with the clank of a monkey wrench. "Gee-min-ee! It's hot under here."

Ten minutes later Uncle George appeared at the head of the table, his hands scrubbed with Lava soap, his hair combed and plastered with a bit of Vitalis. That was my signal to stock his quart glass with ice and strain the fresh-brewed tea into it. I might refill it twice during the meal.

He was not a man to hold his patience forever. Once when we cousins were being particularly rowdy as blessing time approached, he squinted, sighed, then bowed his head and, substituting the usual "Bless, O Lord, this food to the nourishment of our bodies and us to Thy service," he roared, "Bless me and my stupid family. Amen!" (Stupid was one of his basic words. All the world was divided into stupid and not-so-stupid people.)

Uncle George had a number of Jeffersonian traits. He was picky where it counted. The story circulates that once, overhauling a Ford station wagon, he caught sight of a speck of dark grease intermingled with white grease on a bearing handed to him. Disgusted, he returned the bearing to the helper with vivid instructions to make it perfect before he would install it.

Like Thomas Jefferson, he was a tinkerer. If he couldn't fix something, he would design and build a substitute. And sometimes he played at his work. Once he built an entire car starting with an old Ford chassis. His sacred cow was a '49 Studebaker allowed to graze for 30 years in a pasture behind his house. It was rumored Uncle George had been caught talking to it on occasion.

He had the makings of a true pioneer, delivering to the area where he planted himself the best that was in him to do. He was the only one around with a disc roller and would go to the wheat fields to sharpen plows. During wheat harvest, he was on call twenty-four hours a day in the fields to keep the combines humming for miles around. In the years of the Washita Reclamation Project, it was his pride to keep the giant earth-moving machinery operative.

Of all Uncle George's traits, the one the family most remembers him for was, peculiarly, how he *didn't* talk. He extended the meaning of the First Amendment by exercising his right to silence. He could sit quietly in a living room of friends or relatives for two hours and never bother opening his mouth. He wasn't shy: he simply chose not to talk. When I asked Aunt Irene to help me remember some of the things he used to say, she looked at me as if I'd asked her to speak Chinese. "Say?" she asked. "Say?"

He was other things besides a mechanic. He was the Sunday School superintendent of the thirty-four member Gem Community Church. He could also take up the offering, pray morning prayer, announce hymns, and read scripture.

For thirteen years he was a county commissioner of Hemphill County. He got in his Ford and roared all over the county supervising new roads and other projects.

He drove like a lot of Panhandlers do, hell-for-leather. He didn't intend to be reckless, but it just took so long to get anywhere if you drove like the rest of the nation. Once, when we overtook and passed a slow poke doing 70 on a hill, I asked how he knew we wouldn't meet a car head-on at the top. He gazed at me for what seemed like an eternity (Oh God, please make him look at the road!) and said, "'Cause I checked back there at the top of the last hill and nothing was coming." Simple. Of course.

It went against our clan mythology that anything like cancer would challenge Uncle George, so we were astounded when there was an episode of bleeding, surgery, a second surgery, and a summer of chemotherapy. His family gathered at his bedside repeatedly until finally, he arose weakly, said no thank you to another round of chemotherapy, and told everyone to get back to his and her own business.

Talk about freedom of choice! Next he bought a camper and drove it nine hundred miles to the Rio Grande Valley. "I like it down here," he volunteered one day. "Beats those ole ice storms up home all to pieces." And, we thought, it beats going home to die too.

At first he took little walks about the trailer park at sunset with Uncle Charles, his wife's brother— a lifelong friend and now a constant companion.

Then he began on a course of reading his Bible all
the way through. One day he said to me, "Jan, I am
claiming John 14:14–'If ye shall ask any thing in my
name, I will do it.'" I knew better than to ask what
he was asking. Christmas Day he insisted on driving
our extended family of nine in the camper to a
restaurant where he tried his best to join in the
holiday merriment.

In January we asked him almost daily, hinted,
wouldn't he like to go home and see about things?
He lay on the couch and watched ball games
intently, the muscles twitching in his face as he
relived his tackle position on the Oklahoma Baptist
University football team of 1937. (There was a standing joke at class reunions that classmates' athletic
careers were ended when George tackled them during scrimmage.)

"Too cold up there," he'd say. "I'm not stupid."

So we let him lie in the Tioga and watch his tiny
television. We brought him chicken and Aunt Irene
cooked pinto beans for him, his favorite food, and
sat beside him crocheting an afghan.

He lost weight and coughed and rubbed his arms
and finally, he conceded to leaning on a folding chair
when he walked around outside. But he didn't want
to go home.

Then he didn't walk anymore, just sat by the
doorway of the camper. On a so-so day to us
natives, he relished the Valley sun warming his big
gaunt frame.

And he waited for the Super Bowl. That Sunday
he reported, "I have felt better in my lifetime," but
appeared at our house three hours early to get in

position. His daughters remembered the time all 210
pounds of their father turned a somersault on the
living room floor to celebrate the narrow victory of a
Dallas Cowboys' play-off.

A week after Super Sunday, I got an early
morning call. Uncle George had had a stroke in the
night, harsh reminder of his spreading cancer. "Shall
I call the doctor, an ambulance?"

"Oh gosh no," Uncle Charles said. "He finally
wants to go home so we're going."

At noon I went to tell him goodbye. He com-
plained that his arm tingled and his mouth
didn't work right. He stumbled when he tried to get
up. Aunt Irene had fixed him a milkshake and
trickled it down his paralyzed throat.

He held my hand. "We're going home a different
way," he said slowly, "so I can see a little of Texas
I haven't seen." I bent to kiss him. "Goodbye,
favorite niece," he said. Tears pooled in his eyes
and his body heaved with sobs. It was the silent
gruff uncle's supreme gift to the little girl who had
refilled his tea glass long ago.

Ten days later he was dead.

So what does Uncle George's life have to do with
the Fourth of July? I like to think there are many,
many Uncle Georges out there living the good free
American life as he did. Taking advantage of their
right to close up shop and go turkey-hunting.
Opting for a high lonely hill and a gas station.
Refusing to fire a county worker close to his
retirement. Paying for the education of a boy from
Rhodesia. Singing "Amazing Grace" and "How Great

Thou Art" on Sunday mornings. Buying a chord organ and playing it, with a silly little self-conscious laugh, "for the heck of it."

He lived and worked and loved just as he pleased, but he never denied anyone else his unalienable rights because of those druthers. He was decent to men and women and children and animals and God. And vehicles of every age, race, and creed.

Uncle George left big tracks up on the High Plains. He took Life, Liberty, and the Pursuit of Happiness seriously. He was so free to be ordinary that he was extraordinary.

Pick out the Uncle George of your family. He won't have the same characteristics as my Uncle George. He may be small and talk a lot. He may be a professional man in a big city. He may be Aunt Georgette. But in some way he'll remind you of freedom, of the quintessential "American character." He's who he is because he's been allowed to live a life of choices, in a land of choices. And he takes full advantage of that freedom, including holding it in sacred trust. He is all simple joy and simple responsibility. He is the wonderful little person in whom lies the greatness of America.

Uncle Sam by any other name is Uncle George.

SHOULDER TO SHOULDER

Not long ago, the fashion czars decreed skinny sloping unprotected shoulders back "in." Over my padless body!

A few women friends and I have begun a support group for shoulder pad wearers. We're calling ourselves SPUF, Shoulder Pads' United Friends, and it's our aim to defend shoulder pad rights, to offer haven to the deltoid-challenged. Our motto is: "Shoulder Pads are Shoulds."

SPUF is dedicated to preserving the NFL look. We like the illusion of an imposing upper body, not to mention how giant shoulder pads make a hefty waist almost disappear. We're working toward a new definition of "WASP."

Is the fashion world asking men to give up their shoulder pads? How about giving up food instead? Men came out of the original cave wearing healthy shoulders, but pads are still *de rigueur* for their jackets and suits. Always have been, always will be.

Men are nothing if not wise to power. Humphrey
Bogart in his neat square tweeds looking like Eraser
Man—that sort of thing. Okay, so Arnold
Schwartzenegger doesn't always wear shoulder pads?
He's been declared a special category and perma-
nently excused. Frankly, to my eye he needs them
most of all since like most hunks, he's all downhill
from his neck. The slopes are not appealing to me.

Males of any species aren't about to give up
shoulders. Take the male Gambian epauleted bat.
He hangs upside down on a tree limb and unfurls
tufts of white hair on each shoulder, waiting there in
all his shoulder-padded glory until some batty little
female comes by and says, "Hmmm, what interesting
deltoids you have!" Kazzammm! It's all over.

Now women have discovered the psychological
effectiveness of shoulder pads. In the movie *Big
Business*, Lily Tomlin loses the cool executive image
she's working for before her board of directors when
one shoulder pad gets loose and drifts down the arm
of her see-through sleeve.

The other day I was asked to speak to a group,
so I wore my standard black-jacket-with-shoulder-
pads. As I waited the long while before my turn,
the air conditioning waned. I began to fan myself
with my program.

"Take off your jacket," my seatmate urged.

"I can't," I whined. "I won't be power-dressed.
They won't listen to me."

When shoulder pads were at the peak of their
popularity, they were outrageously priced. One
Christmastime some years back, a daughter-in-law
and I figured out how to make them, thinking we'd

fashion a few pairs to upgrade our less powerful garments. What started out as a modest effort to curb the price of glamour and incidentally strengthen togetherness turned into an orgy of shoulder pad making. We sewed enough shoulder pads to supply both teams in the Super Bowl.

We cut three different patterns from the handiest things nearby, Christmas cards. We ended up with a thin little coquettish wedge, for sweaters and blouses, cut from a card proclaiming "Joy"; a medium all-purpose Brillo pad made from "Peace"; and an industrial-strength cornerstone we dubbed "Triumph."

My daughter-in-law went home but I kept on making shoulder pads. I simply couldn't stop. They were mindless little projects to stave off the guilties for watching TV all evening. My daughter-in-law placed her orders long-distance. "I need one pair of red Joys, two pink Peaces, and one basic black Triumph." Are we talking new meaning to Christmas?

Shoulders happen to be one of the most neglected parts of the body. It's true they maneuvered their way provocatively in peasant blouses and off-shoulder evening gear through a couple of decades of Hollywood. But really now, after they've caught an eye, aren't they kind of passive?

About all shoulders can *do* is be smoothed and kissed. Shoulders just, excuse the expression, hump there on either side of the neck. They're bookends for the head, a place to change the direction of the body. Shoulders are in the same category as nape of neck and crook of knee—erogenous zones, sure, but then what?

Soooo, they've got to be played up, and that's what Shoulder Pads' United Friends is all about. We know we're co-dependents and we want to keep it that way. We need each other for support, specifically each other's shoulder pads to cry on. When we meet we practice "I" messages: "*I* think you look better in shoulder pads." "*I* know *I* look better in them one day at a time."

If we work hard, we can have chapters all over the country, but we know we're going to have to keep our shoulders to the wheel.

And for that we will need padding.

 JUST BILL ME

Time was, a bill was a bill. It was even marked BILL on the envelope. No more.

Now we look through a little oblong window to see ourselves addressed. And, strangely enough, we all have the same title: CAR-RT SORT. Next we tear, but carefully, where we're told to, and at this a sheaf of flyers pitches into our laps showing how we can make our lives more fun with diamond pendants, lighted screwdrivers, perfume, and duffel bags. When we reach a white or blue sheet with rows of numbers, we know we've found the bill.

Now we can decide whether we pay the amount listed before or after the surcharge, the net or the gross, the minimum balance or the total to avoid additional charges. We are asked to consider life insurance, check savings plans, look into totally new concepts, notify our congress person, pay our neighbor's light bill, and contribute to college educations.

The company wants to know if we are over 50 years of age, if we smoke, drink, have children, want to provide extra security for our families. We may be told somewhere to deduct last month's charges if the bill and our recent payment inadvertently crossed. We may be confided to, that the competitor is price gouging at this troubled time but that our company is toeing the line.

That's for starters.

Next we're asked to write our account number on our check and to make the check out to some foolish acronym like SNORTFO. (Did research analysts ever consider how weird it is to write a cursive "Exxon" rather than a good old "Humble"?)

If we were smart last month and bought the lighted magnifying glass for only $49.99 or $13 a months for four months, it may have arrived in time for us now to read the incredibly small announce-ment at the bottom of the page which tells us that from time to time the company has the opportunity to share our names with other companies who they deem have products that would make our lives happier. Facts to the contrary?

We are to get up from our bill-paying place, find a sheet of 8 1/2 X 11 white paper and print the words I DO NOT WANT TO RECEIVE VITAL LIFE-SAVING INFORMATION FOR ME AND MY FAMILY, sign it, and return it in a separate envelope marked "Att: Mail Room Specialist."

If the battery has not played out on our magnify-ing glass by now, we can read further that the inter-est rates have been *adjusted* to reflect something-or-other (God knows, never *raised!*) on our outstanding balance. The rationale for this will be perfectly apparent to the Harvard MBA. All the rest of us, suck up and pay the figure in the square.

We notice that our full-credit MONEY card has been sold to yet another bank, this time in Chicago. It has been owned by friendly banks in Houston, Dallas and Minneapolis over the last year. And just to think, when we applied for it, we thought we were doing business with our local bank.

On the home stretch now, we have to consider that this is the *only* statement we will receive, that the P.O. will not deliver unstamped mail, that the address must be showing through the window, and that we are dumb to send cash through the mails. Just before we lick the envelope, we are told to write our full name and address, account number, expiration date, and to indicate whether the above is a new address.

Licking the flap to close the envelope is such a simple maneuver. All we have to do is be sure not to cut our tongues. But wait! It seems the glue won't stick to the colored picture on the back of the envelope which shows the whole family enjoying their new camping equipment.

At this point, we might consider taking our pup tents, our trusty high-beam emergency three-way rotating traffic lanterns, which we obtained for only $89.99 or $17 a month for six months, and heading for the woods where there ain't no bills.

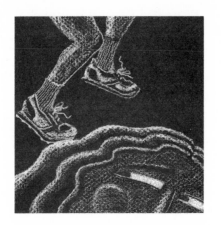

Taking A Run At Joggers

Recently I surprised myself by compli-
menting one of my friends on how sweat-free he
looked sitting at his desk. I had not seen him for a
long time except half-naked, dripping and exhausted
on his homeward lap as I went out each morning.
He was startled too but accepted the remark
graciously, opining that it was too bad I couldn't see
him when he started out—smiling, kissing the wind,
his ultra-dry in control.

Runners tend to be dead earnest about their craft.
I admire runners. Some of my best friends are
runners. I am even a bit envious of them. Still, right
up there with alcohol and double-trailers, they are a
threat on our roadways.

A driver sees a person staggering down the
roadside with just a modicum of clothing, head
bound, body dripping wet, breathing heavy, and the
look on his face one of deep pain or catatonia. Here
is a double for the character in the Bible story on

which the Good Samaritan practiced his art and immortalized himself. It doesn't mean any such of a thing in modern America. The driver must say to himself, "Steady there. It's okay, sport. Don't stop. We got a jogger."

The joggers I see are *always* returning from their farthest point. They have not only passed through runner's high but have slogged on through the valley of the shadow of death by the time I meet them. Each appears to be in the last 10 yards of his life or the Boston Marathon, whichever comes first.

The depth of concentration of these people has long been fare for cocktail party patter. Personally, I think they're willing themselves to stay alive. One I see regularly on his homeward stride admitted his mantra at that point was "leeee-mon-aaaaade."

The other dangerously distracting thing about runners is their peculiar running styles. There are, to my observance, three kinds of runners. One of these moves everything from the waist down. The feet swing out in fancy configurations, the knees goose step, and the buttocks unabashedly compete with each other.

The opposite kind looks as though she were trying to keep from running. She wants to get her upper torso somewhere but must do so through the painful means of moving her feet. She slings her head, pumps and flaps her arms, and twists compulsively at the waist. She seems to be taxiing down a runway with no hope of becoming airborne.

The third type is a combination of the other two, the runner whose every body part that can move, does. These people are doing the necessary running for the rest of the world. No doubt they run with imaginary spear in hand, seeing the antelope just ahead. They are the meat-getters in the great collective unconscious, descendants of stick men frescoed on cave walls in France.

Despite their distracting characteristics, runners possess something the rest of us lazier or less fortunate folk don't: a primary body activity which may be performed in public without disgrace. Eating is sedentary, indoors, and somewhat private; sex is a private thing; and sleeping is downright inert and uninteresting.

But running—ah, here's a flexing body saying hurrah for speed, muscle, motion, for the slap, slap, slap of feet against the earth's surface. A jogger wins a wonderful little Olympiad against inertia every time he runs, and that's doing a lot in a world where competition is often exploitative and ugly.

A Bird? A Plane? An Aviophobe!

Not hypsophobia (fear of high places), hodophobia (fear of travel), tachophobia (fear of speed), or claustrophobia (fear of confined spaces) can explain why more than twenty million of us Americans have aviophobia, fear of flying.

As for me, I like to stand on the edge of canyons, I like to travel, I get a bang out of going 700 mph, and I'd volunteer as an extra in a stuck-elevator episode. But my most vividly-recalled movie scene is the smoldering teddy bear in *The High and the Mighty*; I have prayed for Armageddon or the Second Coming—whichever wants to be first—the night before a flight, and once on board, I've been known to sip the peanuts and crunch the drink.

Still, given the chance on my application to a hereafter, I'll list "flying" as one of the greatest pleasures of my mortal existence. Some things in life are worth being ambivalent about. Flying is one.

I am firmly opposed to anti-aviophobia schools

with their cute aerodynamic explanations and graduation flights. People have every right to be shaky-kneed, pinch-lipped, white-knuckled when they fly. For a long time, I steadfastly resisted flying anywhere, convinced that if God had intended humans to fly, he would have named everyone Icarus and given them flaps on their elbows and small rubber tires at the ends of their legs. My reason for taking the plunge (ah, every cliché has noxious overtones to the aviophobe) was a cousin's wedding a number of years ago.

Sandy was just home from Rhodesia where she'd spent two harrowing years in the bush helping God at a mission hospital. I felt nasty and little to refuse to fly from the Rio Grande Valley to Dallas for her wedding, especially when she had invited our youngest son to be ring bearer. Also, at about that time my job began demanding I be in the Valley on Wednesday afternoon and in Albuquerque or Nashville on Thursday morning. No one living in the last vertebra of the tail of the United States can afford the luxury of being afraid to fly. So, with several nights of fiery-crash fantasies burning in my sleepless head, I took my son's sweaty little hand in my sweaty little hand and headed for the airport.

To feel anything less than pain for a child's illness is unworthy, but I must say I had a twinge of comfort when said son chose to faint in the stuffy terminal lounge as we waited to board. Here was someone more scared than I. Masking my nerves by bathing his face and telling him we simply *had* to make the flight or we'd ruin the wedding, I took his hand and we sprinted through the tube into the waiting plane.

That first flight was memorable, not because of the several moments of disembodiment I experienced wondering if the knees I noticed at the ends of my thighs were mine, nor because the man in our adjoining seat smoked on my pale, nauseated son the whole way, but because we shared the plane with the entire basketball team from Pan American University on its first lap of a trip to Hawaii. For a long time after that, I thought that most air passengers hung their legs over the seat in front of them, chewed bubble gum, and lobbed *Mads* and *Playboys* back and forth across the aisle.

Since that auspicious beginning, I have developed certain rituals to see me through flight trauma. I notice every commonplace item in the flight lounge before take-off: smoking stands, tacky plastic umbrellas, greasy paper bags. I count the number of people reading romance novels. I take great comfort in passive babies sucking pastel bottles of apple juice. My logic is, the more common the surroundings, the less chance of the uncommon.

I do not study people biting their lower lips or staring off into space. I move away from geezers in plaid pants and green patent-leather golf shoes who want to tell me about their night flight aboard a hospital plane from Majorca. I do not look at anyone with his hands in his pockets.

I let float through my brain certain phrases like "four billion air-safety miles per day," "in the unlike-ly event this should become necessary," and "so just sit back and relax." I round out this hypnotic thera-py by recalling the statement of my gung-ho

flying friend who has said on more than one
occasion, upon alighting from my car at the airport
after 30 miles of freeway, "*Now* the *dangerous* part
of the trip is over."

I do not let myself think the once-frightening
thought I had that the mirrored walls in the
passageways from the terminals to the planes are so
you can have one last chance to improve the posture
of your corporeal self: shoulders back, toes pointed
straight, tummy tucked—a sort of last opportunity to
please Mother.

Once I settle in a seat, I begin to think of
frivolous things, such as whether my host at the
other end will notice that I smell like rum if I have
two rum-and-cokes instead of one, whether there is a
talent scout or fashion model or oil field worker or
fertilizer salesman on the plane, whether I have a
sufficient supply of gum should we circle Chicago for
an hour, and whether this will be the flight when I
defy my sister's panty hose rule: Do not answer any
natural bodily urges on a plane because it would be
embarrassing to be found dead at the crash site with
one's underwear around one's knees.

Waiting for take-off, I observe the servicing. Are
they carrying off garbage? If so, this plane has
already been somewhere today, proved itself.

Are the pilot and an attendant smiling while they
converse? They stayed up late playing the slots
together last night in Las Vegas.

Once during my personal pre-flight check, my
bloodhound nose picked up the scent of burning
rubber. When I mentioned it to the attendant, she
told me I definitely did not smell burning rubber, but

if I did, the captain had taken care of it. In other words, Shut up before you get everyone around you nervous.

Air passengers who talk during taxiing or take-off should be muzzled. Everyone knows it takes countless prayers ascending in unison to get tons of airplane aloft. I really never believe it can happen because I don't understand it, even though I've had aerodynamics explained to me. As far as I'm concerned, it's sheer luck and the modern equivalent of an Old Testament miracle every time a plane rises into the air.

But God is not the only deity present with me during flights. The devil often intervenes with a long list of harrowing tales. He reminds me of the baling wire that got sucked into a turbo-prop. Or the coyote that ran across the runway in Lubbock.

I know for a fact the devil is directly responsible for the macabre idea of naming airports after people who died in plane crashes, like Wiley Post Field and Will Rogers Airport. At least one of Satan's emissaries thought up the idea of putting a commemorative plaque in the front of first class, one which proudly states that this airship was ten years old on March 25, 1990 and thus is honored by being named "The Santa Maria." They push cars off cliffs when they're ten years old.

Ever noticed that the outer glass of an airplane window is scratched? Don't. Ever thought that just the paint on a big commercial airline weighs a couple of hundred pounds? Don't. Ever consider that the circumference of a plane tire is just a little larger than that of a bicycle tire? Forget I asked that.

Flights to exotic places have a distinct flavor of the New Year's Eve party scene from *The Poseidon Adventure*. "Just get on. This is the last flight we're going to try to get through today," said a greasy-haired, red-eyed attendant in Denver when I explained I was an hour early for the commuter flight, didn't have a boarding pass, but sure would like to go on to Aspen if the plane wasn't filled up.

There tend to be a lot of peasant blouses, tiger-eye bolos, and carry-on piñatas on planes going north with me out of the Valley. I tolerate these items a good deal better than I did the mess of salmon I got to experience sensorially, courtesy of my seat partner, between Fairbanks and Anchorage.

The jingle of quarters on flights to Las Vegas rivals the roar of the engines. One flawless October day such as only the West can call up, as we flew toward Vegas, the captain came on to tell us if we'd look off to the left, we'd see the Grand Canyon and Boulder Dam. Now to see the Grand Canyon five miles below on a clear October day is a sufficient epiphany for a lifetime. How this directive was followed immediately by one from the attendant requesting everyone to pull down his shades so we could watch the afternoon movie, *Shaggy Dog D.A.*, is a study in the American character.

Thank you, Mr. Hyde. But what of the good Dr. Jekyll? What can be said for the incredible pleasure even an aviophobe can experience aloft? From the vantage of 25,000 feet, features of the landscape are ironed out, tamed to two dimensions by a stern compulsive housekeeper with a muscular ironing arm. Here is the earth laid out like a crazy

quilt: huge circles of Kansas wheat, red-orange
Oklahoma river bottom lands, rich black corduroy
sections of central Texas cotton fields. One wonders
if the farmer knows how great an artist he is.

If everything else is pressed flat, the roads are
not. On a clear day, long straight roads from El Paso
to Lubbock seem to spike upward, making
themselves by *trompe l'oeil* into flagpoles.

The water of this earth has its own set of tricks,
from the quicksilver wink of a swimming pool in
Dallas to the brown winding snake of the Mississippi.
A rivulet increases to a brook, a creek to a river, the
river riots across a road, another road says excuse me
for fifty miles, and the river barrels down, exploding
trees along its banks until from the air, the watershed
looks like an espaliered plant on a Spanish wall.

Tidewater pools along the Gulf shore shine, their
magenta interchanging with glaucous greens like
giant shifting amoebas. Padre Island is a coy
Victorian gathering the lace of waves about her neck.

Once, flying home on the last flight out of
Houston before Hurricane Allen hit in August of 1980
(Don't ask why I was flying in hurricane weather), I
had a chance to see the chimerical nature of water
and sky. The mood in the waiting area in Dallas was
strange, the sober passengers seriously worried, the
drunk ones in torpor or hysteria. All the sane
passengers had canceled.

No plane I've ever been on flew more smoothly
than that one headed into a hurricane. By the time
we reached the Gulf, the hurricane seemed to be
some media ghoul invented for the dog days of
summer. Still, I looked down, half-expecting to see

"heavy seas." There the ocean lay: benign, resplendent in iridescent greens and blues, the eternal pleasant froth of shoreline.

About that time, the captain welcomed us to Flight 51, as captains are wont to do when it's time to land. He told us it was partly cloudy in Harlingen, 78 degrees, wind gusting to 25 mph. As we stared out the west side of the plane, studying the placid coastline and congratulating ourselves on our bravery, he said, "And now, ladies and gentlemen, if you'll look out to the southeast, you will see Hurricane Allen approaching."

We swiveled like a flock of water fowl, and yes, there in the sky were huge roiling black clouds, towering higher than our view would allow us to take in. Lady, I mouthed, looking back at the beautiful lacy Gulf, you're in for a surprise.

The heart at four or five miles up has a tendency to laugh at its own silly beating. Trying to imagine a presence in a farm shed, or in a clump of trees, then imagining being in that clump, maybe having a picnic, maybe getting a car started, I realize that I am, after all, just a single cell, really not even enough to have anyone's eyes trained on. And I smile at the freedom inherent in a total lack of importance.

On a flight, I often take a poll of those around me. No one else is smiling. Most aren't even looking out. They are reading the *Wall Street Journal* or eating peanuts. A mother is changing a baby.

Sometimes a line from a psalm memorized at Baptist Vacation Bible School springs out of nowhere:

"The heavens declare the glory of God and the firmament shows forth his handiwork." Yes, that's it: the ground shows what God can do but the heavens show the *glory,* the *is,* not just the *can do.*

Maybe it's the altitude, but just for an instant, I could slip my seat belt, ease into the aisle as if I were on my way to the lavatory, and start dancing. Dancing on an airplane is a subversive activity. I think better of it.

Sealed in this silver tube, away from the cuts and bruises of earth, away from the stacks of memos, the line of ants trooping through the grass, the No. 8 package of round-head screws from the hardware store, I ask myself if this is a little of what God sees, turning a deified eye and blinking during off-hours. The splendor, the love for all things—clouds, earth, self, other small and finite beings—comes on without mercy.

Outside, more mashed potatoes, these etched in butter by the sun. Okay, okay. The aviophobe surrenders, for a few heavenly minutes, to the aviophile.

Stumbling Onto Something True

"Close your eyes: Smell tennis shoes in your P.E. locker... now a roast burning...now chlorine in the town swimming pool."

Around the U-placed tables my class of life story writers rustles. It's been a morning about memory. They're calling it quits for today—folding notebooks, winding tape recorder cords, capping pens.

The last tip for the day: Visit a museum with a contemporary. Julia raises a braceleted arm. "What if all your girlfriends have gone to the Great Slumber Party in the sky?" Someone like Julia always plays into my hand.

"A good point. But they don't have to be your grade school chums, only someone with a common experience."

Inge speaks from one side of the "U". She was once blonde, retains in her eyes the crystal azure of her northern European heritage. "No one I can find who would wish to go back with me to my history.

I spend my childhood in Berlin in the war."

Two or three of the group let out the barest of sighs.

"I say did you now?" chimes Elisabeth, suddenly alive across from her. "I spent my childhood also in the war. But in London."

"And was there darkness and shattered glass, and the sounds of the sirens all day long?" asks Inge.

Fingering a strand of white hair near a weather-blushed cheek, Elisabeth answers, "All those."

"We gather shrapnel in our aprons, play with it in doorways," Inge says, "under beams that are broken."

"An unexploded bomb was jolliest," Elisabeth says. "When we discovered it, we would race at once to the war ministry office, screaming the entire way."

Now the class sits like tennis spectators, quietly looking back and forth in rhythm. "Yes, and what did we think, that we get a prize?" asks Inge.

"It must have been for the joy of running."

There's a pause. "Your father did what?"

"Royal Air Force. Bomber pilot."

"Mine too," Inge says, then blushes, "I mean—the Luftwaffe."

The room is quiet. Elisabeth finally speaks. "Then . . . excuse me, but I believe that . . . our fathers were bombing each other . . . "

"And us." Inge finishes.

"Commonality of experience." It's all I can muster by way of dismissal, and that seems too much. Then lighter, I call after them, "Next time is our last class. Anybody who wants to bring a goodie is welcome to."

When we meet again, Elisabeth comes early, sets on the desk a plate covered with a white eyelet tea towel. Underneath, the shortbread is light gold, with an embossed bouquet design in the middle, cut in wedges enough for all.

Inge is late. She bears a box. It's filled with a double jeopardy of chocolate—*schokoladen stückchen* with *streusel* sprinkled on top. She's brought napkins for the inevitable delectable mess.

At the end of this last day, when I have said everything I know to encourage them to finish their life stories, we pass the offerings around.

Elisabeth's shortbread snaps with butter and sugar, showering crumbs into our laps. The chocolate petits fours are as profligate as the shortbread is pristine.

We lick our fingers of Inge's gift, touch their dampness to our laps to collect Elisabeth's crumbs.

"Fifty years," someone says quietly.

We look anxiously at Inge, at Elisabeth. They are gazing across the tables at one another, smiling shyly.

A large but not uncomfortable silence seals us as we take this communion.

AND THE ROCKET'S RED GLARE

There is nothing neutral about fireworks. Our associations with them are agony or ecstasy, with little between.

Who among us does not have a firecracker memory bank? My earliest is an agony, the news that one of my playmates had been torched in his father's fireworks warehouse. Even then, there was a mystery about fireworks. No one in our little north Texas community felt adequate for pronouncing the family's foreign-sounding name; the boy had black curly hair and eyelashes I envied; and I couldn't understand his words at times. Firecrackers came from somewhere else, maybe gypsies. They were magic.

Later, on a July night when a double-date lit a cherry bomb and failed to get it out the window of the car in time, four of us scared kids rode 30 miles over the cap rock at high speed to get the hand of our moaning buddy put together again.

In my adult life the pain of fireworks has emanated principally from the agony of our beloved dachshund Taffy every New Year's Eve and Fourth of July for the fourteen years of her life. As others danced the night away or milled about eating cotton candy at town celebrations, we sat home with our hands over the ears of a quivering, flare-eyed little brown bundle of canine nerves scootched between us on the couch.

But then there's the ecstasy. The package of one hundred Black Cats, with their Chinese-y red paper backing, their fuses intertwined, to be shared with brothers and sisters and cousins. The little green tanks that shoot across the sidewalk . . .Stand back!

The dancing girls . . . Ooh-la-la!

The sparklers . . . Look! Look, everybody! My name in lights!

One summer a young visitor from Scotland came to our home over the Fourth. Malcolm was obsessed with fireworks. It seems his favorite holiday was Guy Fawkes Day, celebrated Nov. 5 in the British Isles. In 1605, Guy Fawkes and his friends were prepared to blow up the English Parliament because of its intolerance to Catholicism. The plot was discovered, Parliament saved, and Guy Fawkes and his fellow plotters executed a few days later.

From his perch in the anti-heroes' section of the Hereafter, Guy Fawkes would be glad to know that he made quite an impression on a family in South Texas in the twentieth century. Because children are not allowed fireworks in Scotland, our visitor Malcolm spent his entire American allowance on firecrackers. In a frenzy of international goodwill, the son who was designated as Malcolm's playmate followed suit. The buying got out of control, which necessitated trip after trip to the countryside to try to expend the firecracker purchases.

Finally Malcolm went back to Scotland, leaving his inadmissible leftovers with us. Our son abandoned his supply in favor of the next summertime diversion. What was to be done with leftover firecrackers? We were probably the only family in South Texas with a two-year supply of Roman candles and Black Cats in the vegetable drawer of the refrigerator.

With city ordinances prohibiting fireworks in town, many of us confine ourselves to watching the magnificent display our city sponsors each year in the high school stadium on the evening of the Fourth.

Fireworks watching is a communal thing. Who wants to say "Aahhh!" and "Oooh, lookathat!" to one's self? We often get together with another family, the McLeods, with whom we've been friends many years, either in their yard or ours. After hamburgers and homemade ice cream, we settle in, "about dark-thirty" as the farmers say, chairs arranged in a semi-circle, mosquito goop generously applied.

At first we had our collective six young boys near us, closely supervised with their sparklers and penny-poppers. Lately, they have come home on the Fourth from college or jobs, to lie stretched at our feet, indulging us with their presence. They balance their drink cans on their stomachs and call each other "Dude" for old times' sake. They regale us in deep murmuring voices with stories of their long-ago

exploits with fireworks—tales about bottles and cans,
about altered wicks and fuses. They think us mellow
enough for the particulars of close calls and near
misses, admitting their childhood terrors and fantasies
about fireworks.

All the while our heads are tilted upward, eyes
trained on the beautiful South Texas night sky. We
know that a shower of multi-colored lights does not
countenance inattentiveness. At first they come
slowly—a dandelion puffball of red, an alternate
burst of green nearby, a few diamond-white Pows!
In between, we look to the south where an adjacent
town's display has begun.

After a while, the pace picks up, with four or five
formations at once. Now the fancy ones commence
and they bear exclamation and description: "Look!
That one's three colors!" "That one just keeps
popping!" "Oooh, they're coming down like rain!"

A few charge up with a promising whistle . . .and
fizzle out, dropping silently and darkly to their
ignominious death. We are sorrowful, with a tinge of
smugness that even stellar actors sometimes fail.

It's nearly ten o'clock. A few moments go by
with no more activity. A pall of smoke meanders
northward. A childish primitive disappointment starts
to gather in us. "Nothing gold can stay." Someone
quotes Frost's line and stands to fold his lawn chair.
One or two remain perfectly still.

Then the whole sky lights with rockets, flares,
bursts. There's rat-a-tat-tat and booooom! Diamonds
and emeralds and sapphires spray from their nuclei
in perfect symmetry, birthing little secondary jewels.
Some linger a milli-second, asking if they might be

stars too. Others ride gravity home, whistling as they go. We stand transfixed in our leave-taking, a lawnful of statues. The excessiveness floods us with pleasure. Then it's over.

A longtime friend, Peggy Steiner, tells a grand story of an intergenerational firecracker event in Salina, Kansas. It seems that the year Peggy was five, her Grandmother Needels came to Salina from a remote farm to live with the family.

As was his practice on the Fourth, Peggy's father bought a large box of firecrackers and, with the family assembled on the front porch, handed them out one by one, letting each child by turn light them until they were all gone. This event was greatly anticipated and if they were careful, they could make it last a couple of hours. On this particular Fourth, Grandmother Needels was seeing and hearing her first firecrackers.

A few moments into the festivities, Dad struck a match to light a punk, a spark flew into the box of firecrackers, and the family's supply of butterfingers, sparklers, Roman candles, and pinwheels detonated in one glorious boom and flash. The children and parents were mute with shock, but Grandmother Needels rose to the occasion. "That was a nice BIG one!" she said sweetly.

Fireworks by their very nature involve all ages. Maybe that's one reason we like them so much: we're all *there* for them—hooting, hollering, worrying, warning, teaching, admiring—everybody from the lap baby to the grandma.

As the exclamation marks of liberty, the rocket's red glare reminds us that living in a democracy, despite its occasional duds, its latent danger and excessive noise, is cause for celebration. That for the availing ourselves of it, liberty may fill us with light and joy.

Sepia Print

Christmas in Arkansas with my grand-parents—a montage of memories. There were certain things in that lumbering early-Federal hilltop house that assured us we had survived another year: a papier maché reindeer with one prancing paw amputated sitting under the Christmas tree, a crystal bowl filled with chunks of cracked peppermint, pine cones lying in slightly dingy cotton snow on the long table in the hall below the picture of the Roman Colosseum.

The dinner table on Christmas day was set with a mixture of all available plates. Cousins ate at the corners. There was an aunt who couldn't eat any dressing because she was allergic to sage. I remember the delights coming from jars brought from the mysterious storm cellar—cloyingly sweet amber-colored pear preserves, apple butter, pickled peaches. There were turnip greens and creamed corn and sweet potatoes. For dessert, a pound cake

appeared, with nary a touch of rum in it (my grand-
father was a Baptist circuit rider preacher) and
ambrosia in a bowl so big it couldn't be passed
around.

In the afternoon a domino tournament broke out
among the cousins, with periodic time-outs for trips
to the divinity and fudge. Sometimes we played
tunes on my grandmother's Crown reed organ, taking
turns working the pedals. Or we prowled among the
books in Pappaw's study, stuffing silly notes in the
pigeonholes of his roll-top desk for him to explode
over when we were hundreds of miles away.

In the evening, if my grandmother was not too
tired, she'd make us fried apple or peach pies. They,
by themselves, were worth the long drive to
Arkansas. We buttered these pockets of heaven with
churned butter kept in a crystal fluted bowl with a
lid. Everyone fought to be first to disturb the design
Mammaw had wrought on top of the pure golden
mound. Pappaw would take one bite of his pie, rear
back in his hobble-legged cane bottom chair and
declare with authority, "Eh law!" which was his first
and last word on everything. My grandmother would
giggle a bit, smooth a straying wisp of curly gray
hair, and dry her hands on her apron for the hundredth time.

There was no heat in any of the bedrooms and
the plan was to pull on our sleepers before the fire
in the dining room and make a dash for it. Sisters
went in pairs: a bed was too cold for only one to
warm up. Tickling each other and making bicycle
motions with our legs were standard remedy for
frigid sheets. Drowsy, we strained to hear the

grown-ups across the hall laughing about adult things they'd been waiting all day to tell. In the night, I woke long enough to feel the stern admonition of a layer of patchwork quilts, holding me still and telling me to go back to sleep.

Next morning there would be the excruciatingly cold but urgent visit to the outhouse and a stop back by the well to break the thin layer of ice by dashing the bucket against it.

And then I'd enter the steaming kitchen where, no matter the moment, my grandmother would be pulling a pan of her biscuits from the oven of the black wood-burning stove, and insisting she had made these just for me.

It's Time For The Doldrums

Certain things before Christmas cry to be mentioned: holly wreaths, manger scenes, good will. The time after Christmas furnishes its own list of tear jerkers.

In many of us, a post-holiday fit of ill will can be induced by the necessity of cleaning the turkey. Nutritionists tout a turkey's wonderful protein worth, but a turkey is still ten pounds of high quality succulent meat stuck together with ten pounds of slimy ligaments, dagger tendons, and enough grease to lubricate a wagon train.

Lurking in my background somewhere is the Puritan duty to sit down with an old bird carcass and pick off every smidgeon of meat, presumably to make into an alliterative recipe like Turkey Tetrazzini. My mother even boils the carcass after the picking, claiming it delivers tasty soup broth. I'm sorry, Mom, but some family traditions are just not worth preserving. When the "inner basting" has worked its

way to my elbows, I quit. I'm not really big on
being a link in the Food Chain.

Then there's always some soggy leftover dressing
inside the bird. No one has ever, as far as I'm
concerned, been able to come up with a decent
recipe using leftover dressing. Dressing is a
casserole, and mixing a casserole into another
casserole amounts to the same thing as mixing all
the colors: you get gray.

Taking the tree down also produces a lot of anti-
Christian behavior at our house. The world is divided into two groups of tree-takers-down: those who
look on a December 26 tree as criminal evidence to
be disposed of as quickly and discreetly as possible,
and those who insist the tree must stay up until the
second week in January because it's so expensive.

We are in group one, and so, on the morning of
the 26th, the tree is hastily undressed and hauled to
the alley, usually with a small boy riding it.
Meanwhile, back in the house, I begin vacuuming
the swath of dead needles and foil icicles while the
dog sits nibbling the imbedded glitter in her paw.

What really brings on the muttering is to find,
after the stars and elves and angels have gone to
their respective small boxes and all these put into
one big box labeled "Xmas Decor" and this big box
heaved to the top shelf in the utility room—what
really makes me see red is to find we left out the
doorknob cozy Aunt Lilly knitted for us seven years
ago, or to notice a little Santa cup ho-ho-ho-ing on
the counter.

Close following is the onset of mechanical
mayhem. The true nature of gift toys and small

appliances becomes apparent. Batteries die. Plastic dinosaurs suddenly cease ranging over the earth. We begin ranging over the discarded boxes seeking warranty cards and assembly directions. And we realize we are never going to win a game of brain teasers our sons bought us.

We tell ourselves to be philosophical, to understand that mountain-top experiences are possible only because there are valleys between.

And then we secretly thank God for the eleven quiet months ahead before the next orgy of human-designed falderol.

A Nineties Kind of Wedding

Mother goes on honeymoon with SON: NEW WIFE FOLLOWS IN OTHER CAR . . . . Only in the nineties, you say. Not as bizarre as it sounds but definitely a nineties kind of wedding, the kind our family celebrated in the spring of '93.

Enter Groom Avrel, youngest of three sons. The baby the other two are assigned to guard in the shopping basket. The toddler they shout at, the preschooler they snatch gadgets from, telling him he's too dumb to operate them. The little illiterate they draw pictures for, read stories to.

Later, my husband Carl and I notice Avrel's zany streak. He's the second grader who says, "School can ruin your mind," and the fourth grader, who, when beat out by topnotch Susan, observes, "The way I see it, women are going to get better until they finally take over the world."

He is a grade-school expert in killer whales, John Hancock, boxing, the Doobie Brothers. In high school, he becomes the family genealogist, a local rock guitar icon, an orchestral violinist.

Suddenly, this pipsqueak of a little brother is twenty-six years old, six-foot-one, a man in a distant city with a college degree and a responsible job. Turns out he's a traditionalist: he wants a church wedding. Will we help him get married?

Enter Bride Beth, sprung from a duo of sisters in southern Louisiana. She's a yin-yang of values, interests, ideals. Early family pictures show her licking Mommie's cake pan or curled cherubically in a pint-size chaise lounge, eyes hooded and dreamy. She plays Barbie dolls, eats too many of her grandmother's rum balls at Christmas, makes safe harbor in the lap of Ruth, the family housekeeper.

Later, her sturdy, curvy legs will pound the basketball courts on the freshman women's team at L.S.U. And still later, her journalism skills land her an interview with a promising governor from Arkansas. Next, she's under a bridge, with gas mask and flak jacket, covering the Persian Gulf war.

"I can do that," this woman says, when approached about a traditional church wedding. "If I'm supposed to dress up in a long white dress and march down the aisle and stand there a little while, I can do that." Her personal preference would be a justice of the peace on an ordinary day and pocket the difference. But she loves the groom, and her first major concession in the marriage will be The Marriage.

So they're off, with an abstraction at first, something the man had in mind all along, something the woman agrees to tolerate. Something called *wedding.*

Is a wedding an anachronism in the nineties? After all, they've been living together eight months. This I overhear her tell two of my conservative friends when they ask if she's excited about getting married.   Then I remember that the Mbuti tribes of Africa have the couple live together at least a year, sometimes two, before calling them married.

So now I get a book from the library. Seems a Hopi Indian wedding involves a number of ceremonies stretching out over a year. And some of the Canadian Eskimos have trial marriages, lasting about a year, to decide if the couple is going to get along well together. And the Japanese, well . . . on and on.

I close the book on marriages. Get over it, WASP Mother. "We had a first for everything," the groom says to me later, in a conversation about love customs. "The firsts just came in a different order from yours and Dad's."

So after a move to another city, new jobs, new cars, the acquisition of Mutt-and-Jeff dogs and a fixer-upper house, they name a date.

Like a baby suddenly awake and squalling hungry, this event demands attention. Can they have it in our hometown? And could we just sort of go ahead and make a few calls, like to the bakery and the church and the florist, because they have new jobs 350 miles away?

As the social chairperson of our family, the decision falls to me. Ten minutes (outside) and I say yes. Because Carl and I like this young woman—she's special—and we want to have her around. And we like our son and want him to be happy. And because we're an old-fashioned, close, Grapes-of-Wrath "We is the family" kind of family.

So around Christmastime it's put on the calendar, a Saturday evening in May. Well . . . the night before also, for the rehearsal. And people will need to eat that night, so where? Our backyard is penciled in.

And where the reception? We're mulling this over when a friend with a lovely walled garden calls to ask what she might do. She's enlisted.

Suddenly, it's March and I rush to the printer's, back with the samples, the samples off to the nearly-weds, the first of scores of phone calls between the betrotheds and the planners.

Invitations out, there is a sense of no return. A trickle back of "Return to Sender," "Addressee Unknown," "Forwarding Date Expired." What had it taken to get this list? Combing through the last list, the brother's list, I marveled at the changes in our friendships in only five years: this wife is dead, these are divorced, this one has remarried, these have children old enough to attend this time. And I am never quite sure I have done the right thing by inviting this one and not that one, by sending an invitation to an old acquaintance in a distant city. Will they be flattered or dismayed? Will the gesture be interpreted as warm and connecting, or formalistic and greedy?

Now the first gift comes, a place setting of the china the bride has picked. We remember the day after Christmas when she and I went, late in the afternoon, to a local department store and made the selections. She wasn't thrilled that she wasn't thrilled.

A scene of giddy girlfriends ogling china and crystal lunges at her from a bride's magazine. "How am I supposed to know what kind of dishes to get?" wails this nineties woman.

That day I smile all the way to the shopping mall. This is a girl after my own heart. This is how I wish I'd been—upfront, honest, brash—when the soft roses and satin pillows and silver platters came raining down on me in the fifties.

I tell her, "Look, I didn't know anything about dishes and stuff when I got married either. You'll learn, and meanwhile, it's nice to have things picked out when people ask what you need."

In the Bridal Selection Department, Beth musters considerable aplomb for the job. She takes in the difference between Lenox china and Japanese stoneware. She listens to the reason that sterling silver patterns are so ornate. (Silver scratches easily.) She weighs the merits of the lead content of this crystal goblet against the heady design of that one. Then she strikes with lightning speed.

The Bridal Consultant demurs to register anyone a mere two hours before closing, especially on the day after Christmas when Housewares is crowded with dissatisfied gift recipients. How about next week, say, on Thursday?

I check Beth's face. The hard-hitting reporter has climbed into the bride's eyes. I think of the time when, sent to a Mexican federal penitentiary on a reporting assignment, she was held at gunpoint for three hours in an international power play.

She smiles sweetly. "That won't be possible. Give me the papers. Now." The Bridal Consultant instantly complies.

Beth sits down and hovers over the selection list. Every now and then she lifts her head: "How many place settings of this stuff do I want?" "Do I want a butter dish?" "The fluted champagne or the 6-oz. wine—maybe neither?" I answer the best I can.

But now, weeks later, the first gift arrives. And as the bride opens the big silver box, she laughs that she could have been afraid of domesticity. And the groom stands smiling in the background, nonplussed in his secondary role, faintly prescient of the time he will get to handle these dishes in soapy water.

We go on first-name terms with the UPS man after he begins to come every evening at 6 with boxes from Albuquerque, Los Angeles, Mexico.

Now I have a list each morning: baker, rental service, party goods, dressmaker. And at night, the list is only half finished. The next morning, new items appear: call the organist, add this neighbor to the list, drop this swatch by the florist.

It's three weeks to go and the nearly-weds come home for a round of errands, decisions, a wine-and-cheese party with their friends home for Easter. The party is a big success, with a fine comingling of the young people, who by now are not quite so young, and their older parents. It's a time to catch up on who has what new job, new degree, new address, new significant other.

The week before the wedding, time tracks backward in anticipation, forward in responsibility. Lists are still made each morning but now the number of items begins to thin. Where once there was a drive across town, now a phone call will do. And it's just for confirmation, not decision. The crucial stuff is all decided. What will be will be.

We're down to ceramic birds or bride-and-groom miniatures atop the cake. Alone, I opt for the birds, since the miniatures look like disgruntled foreigners. We're down to who, exactly, will pick up the champagne glasses at the rental company on Saturday morning.

Friends call to cajole, sympathize, offer advice and last-minute help. Earlier, they've been signed on to help with the reception. One acquaintance, astonished that we were into a do-it-yourself wedding, said, "You mean you're *catering* your own wedding?" Sometimes now we're astonished too.

We're also not sleeping well. When I awaken at 1 or 2, I begin again on the plan, ending up praying for the safe miles of everyone flooding into the wedding.

Thursday rolls around and we drive to the airport for the minister and his wife, who happen to be the groom's grandparents. Pappaw is 79 and he's been into scrupulous artery maintenance all spring in preparation for officiating at this, his fourth wedding of a grandchild. We're a serious do-it-yourself family.

The bride's parents arrive from Louisiana, bringing with them an entourage of fun-loving friends, and we exchange greetings on the steps of the church before the rehearsal. Inside, we straggle down the darkened aisle in two's and three's to bunch on the front pews and receive instructions for the ceremony.

The two families eye each other with gentle wariness. We aren't exactly powerful clans arranging and bargaining this contract. We are two random American families plucked up from neighboring states by the lottery of love and set down here in a curious late-twentieth-century ceremony. Vestiges of the past: the father practices his give-away speech; a trio of tiny flower-bearing sisters, presaging the bounty of children, is coached down the aisle; attendants are positioned near the bride and groom for aid and succor.

The preacher rehearses the benediction and the organist makes a note of his final words, then flares out with Widor's joyous "Toccata from Symphony No. 5"—a favorite of some of us. The bride stops a few feet from the exit. She turns on her black suede wedgies and calls sweetly down the nave to the organist, "Could we have something else to leave by? That sounds like a skating rink to me." The bride has not exercised her veto privileges nearly as often as she might have. Wish granted.

Now the party adjourns to the house for dinner. It's what we call a western Mexican meal, with potato salad, beans *a la charra*, brisket, sausage, rice, and handmade flour tortillas. The visiting Cajuns compliment the sausage and rice. A cake of strawberries and cream rounds it off and a basket of *leche quemada* candies is passed. We play zydeco tapes for the bride and old Doobie Brothers for the groom. The bride gives Barbie dolls to her little flower girls in a rite of passage that reminds us of the Japanese rite of passage where the bride burns all her toys and playthings.

After dinner, we practice another rite as old as

the Aztecs. Avrel and Beth sit in the backyard spotlight and each guest gives a piece of advice about marriage. We observe that the younger people are concerned with equality in salaries and the distribution of chores; the older folks advise charity and patience.

The wedding day, May Day, dawns sunny, and we breathe a sigh of relief, for just the day before, it had been raining. The morning is taken up with preparing for the reception. At noon we gather for sandwiches at the house, with the bride and groom successfully dodging each other. Then a hush comes over everything.

At three, my sister, her husband, and I drive to a neighboring town to get the wedding cakes. We ride the twelve miles to the reception site with the carrot cake on my lap, the wedding cake balanced on hers.

The groom comes briefly in the afternoon while the bride sequesters herself in the guest room. He gathers up his clothes, the marriage license, his gifts for his groomsmen, and, looking slightly nervous and worried, departs for a friend's.

It's six and the bride emerges to take a bath. I'm nervous we will not make it to the church by seven, where we are to meet the bride's mother and sister and friends for the formal dressing of the bridal party.

At six-thirty, the bride decides to trim her bangs. We gasp, give her the scissors. She does it in thirty seconds flat. I have momentarily forgotten she is an on-camera TV reporter who can do *anything* during a commercial pause. We arrive at the church exactly on time and I urge the bride, dressed in leotards and

T-shirt and with her hands full of various objects, to go on in. I assure her I can manage the wedding dress.

She goes, and for a moment I'm left there alone in the parking lot to tussle with the beautiful white satin dress. Beth trusts me, I think, and it pleases me no end, this mother of boys, about to get another daughter-in-law.

Inside, dress delivered, I leave quickly the domain of mother and daughter and sister. It is their time together.

I go down the hall where Avrel is waiting with his groomsmen. They are an odd mix of nerves and jokes. I look at Ave as though I've never seen him before, for sure will never see him this way again. For once his hair is behaving in front. I fix it just a li-i-i-itle more. He immediately turns to the mirror and re-does what I have done, then grins at me. He's princely in his formal tux with tails. I fight the lump in my throat, remember that tears will smear my make-up.

It's time. The organ has been playing a while. We go out to the narthex. The church is beautiful, with a huge country bouquet of flowers on a pedestal, candles glittering in their candelabra, votive lights winking along the railing. This magic is the gift of Avrel's brother Erren.

Carl and I walk down the aisle and when we sit, it seems that a thousand pounds rises from my shoulders. I involuntarily shudder a little and the relatives behind chuckle quietly.

Not a hitch in the ceremony, not one. Especially touching are the three little girls floating down the aisle in their blue floral dresses, their white baskets filled with creamy roses.

After the kiss, Beth polishes Avrel's lips quickly and gently with her fingertips when she sees she has left her imprint on him. It is a considerate and funny gesture and the audience laughs with them.

At the reception, the moon blesses the courtyard with an illumination of the huge South Texas sky. The cake is cut, the champagne and punch consumed. The guests mill about and no one's too eager to leave. The groomsmen bring in a bust of Elvis with sunglasses as a gift to adorn the new home.

The wedding party visits on and on and the crowd thins a little. The honorees disappear and return in casual dress. Amid flying birdseed (one tired guest forgets and throws the whole bag at them) they dash for their car, a 1969 Ford Mustang convertible loaned by the reception host for the evening. As they pull away, they look like a picture cut from an old Life magazine.

I turn to the car owner. "Oh Don! What a great thing you did!" I blubber. And he and I are swamped in tears.

Hasty goodbyes now and we turn, with the hosts, to the clean-up chores. There's a lot to rearrange, haul, wash, take home. No getting around it.

My *other* daughter-in-law and I fill the trunk with presents. I collect the groom's tux from a side room, all the while thinking how awful my feet feel.

Finally, we're home. Our little grandson Luca, who has borne his two-and-a-half-year-old self

manfully through the evening, goes in search of his
McDonald's Happy Meal sack abandoned hours ago.
He looks at it without luster in his eyes. Then he
turns and goes to the bedroom. He returns to the
hallway, where we're padding up and down, posi-
tions his pillow, lies down, covers himself up, and
closes his eyes. All our sentiments.

So what of this strange thing we have done?
What does it mean, if anything, this nineties
wedding? Is the glue tighter for all our efforts?
Wedding: a thing of uncertain return—happiness
remembered forever, or reminder of grave mistake.

We risk the delirious pleasure of family celebration, and then we wait, hoping for the miracle of
an old-fashioned home, with love and laughter and
perhaps children. We hope, with Homer, for
"nothing nobler or more admirable than when two
people who see eye to eye keep house as man and
wife, confounding their enemies and delighting their
friends."

Oh—but why, why did the mother go on the
honeymoon with the groom? Very simple. The bride
and groom came downstate for the wedding in separate cars so they could take their wedding gifts home
upstate. After a night in the bridal suite of a local
hotel, they surfaced at our house. Enter the mother,
who must fulfill a longstanding workshop date
upstate the following Monday. Her ride has just
fallen through.

"You can ride with me, Mom," the sweet
groom says.

Oh, but, is this okay with the bride?

"Sure," the nineties bride says, "as long as we can

meet at the Dairy Queen in Three Rivers."
And so of course we do.

A LETTER TO A LONG-AGO BOY

D̲ear Son,

Today (or rather yesterday, for now it's 3 a.m. on the day following) you did what you and your friends euphemistically call "wiping out" on your bicycle. Most wiping out involves a long black skid mark on a neighborhood street and a fearsome but innocuous crash to the pavement, for some perfectly logical reason like a dog dashing in front of you or a mechanical failure that locks your brakes.

Only today you wiped out because you and your bicycle, going north, met unexpectedly at the turn into a blind alley, a ton of Pontiac going south. Tonight your bicycle sits propped against the backyard fence, a tangle of gear lines, aimless spokes, and flabby rubber loops you and your dad referred to last week on your way home from the bike shop as tubes and tires.

I am awake now, startled from the first restless sleep of the night into articulate, fundamental prayer, thanks for the umpteenth time that only your bicycle and not you died in the accident.

You lie a few feet away on the guest couch, moving every few minutes, sometimes moaning, sometimes bumping the wall with your sprained knee. You kick out violently the scraped raw foot or carefully favor the bound elbow we gazed into earlier in the emergency room only to confront raw bone and muscle.

Something new hurts every little while, and you rise long enough to identify the painful shoulder, the stiff neck to me, but to refuse, like any sturdy four-teen-year-old, the ice pack or more pain medicine.

I wish I could assure you this sort of thing will never happen again, that you've fulfilled your quota to the monster of random violence, paid your debt to a society of fast things running on awesome power. It might be a miserable lie.

Just as the showers that come off and on now in the night from a rheumy South Texas sky, your life will be punctuated by these splats of fate. I can give you umbrellas of "Be carefuls!" and I can teach you to take advantage of luck and to come in whenever skies threaten. But I can't hold back the rain, much as it's in me as a mother to try.

In a few days you will go forth, almost as good as new, back to school with generous portions of hero pride and nightmare fright, both a little ashamed and a little proud as you tell of your accident. You will forevermore stop at blind alley crossings.

As I sit here aching for you, I ponder my own paradox: that in the near loss of you, dear, my love is renewed. Of course, you know I have loved you always—as moms do easily, but when I saw you hurt, the love came bounding from me almost tangibly, like the bright innocent blood of your wounds—*there* all the time, but suddenly noticeable, calling attention to itself.

So it's like this: When I loved you into being, I took the chance of loss. In every shiny bicycle of life there lies a chance of wiping out. Caring and daring are risky business, but they are about all we can know of that precious beauty we call living.

Until we can talk about it more,

Mom

LOVE A HAMBURGER /
LOVE YOURSELF

I have just eaten my every-so-often deluxe burger from the fast food chain at the end of my street. I had with it a medium cherry coke. The burger was a little cool on top when I got home. After a couple of bites, the juice of the tomato and the mayonnaise ran together down my arm appreciably so that I had to make the *de rigueur* napkin pocket for the thing. After all, I was reading a fresh library book.

The bun was white, but, I told myself, it had proteinic sesame seeds. The lettuce crunched a little and the pickles were fresh. The meat tasted mild and there was something golden near it that I took as a reasonable facsimile of cheese. I salted the burger with the entire contents of one little pouch. And I ate the thing, one bite after another, until it was completely gone. Then I drank my cherry coke.

It was a wonderful meal. I feel as though I've had a little vacation. What's more, I am totally satisfied for five hours.

I know there is everything wrong with what I did: the ground beef (gall stones? tartar in the arteries? breast lumps?), the white bread (death to rats), the mayonnaise and mustard and cheese (faked chemical formulas). Even now, as I write, I grow sleepy and wonder if I should simply pause and let the deadly starch and fat overdose have their way with my eyelids.

And yet, in a few days, I'll need another deluxe fix. I'll jump in my little blue car and barrel down the street, ready to sell my birthright in exchange for a mess of pottage and a cherry coke. I'll hate myself a little that day too as I eat my burger over another library book. A little voice inside me will say, "Ugly American. If you were only French, you'd crave raw mushrooms and baker's bread straight off the back of a bicycle. If you were only Italian, you'd have homemade pasta. Or Chinese. Or Japanese. Then you'd be stuffing down those wonderful chopped things, barely cooked, at 20 calories a half-barrel."

Isn't it time we Americans stopped hating ourselves? Personally I think our overdosing on foreign aid is a result of not loving ourselves very well. Could we give ourselves a break? Could we lay off?

The cherry coke takes me back to another day. I'm on the green leatherette stool at Ramsey's soda fountain in Waxahachie, Texas and I'm watching to see that the soda jerk squirts an ample enough stream of cherry elixir in my glass. Let me die thus watchful.

I for one will rise up and call my occasional

Americanburger and my cherry coke blessed. On special occasions I will get the bacon and avocado burger, with a lime coke to match the avocado. I will *never* get the jiffy-burger: jiffies have no taste; jiffies are un-American.

I will take my witness seriously. I will have the courage not to hide the empty striped sack in the bottom of the kitchen garbage.

Remembering The Sabbath

Home from church on Sunday night in Waxahachie, my sister and I slammed our Bibles on the dresser, shed our crinolines, and stepped out of our ballerina slippers. Dad took off his shoes and wriggled his toes in the carpet. He unsnapped the sock garters that kept his bare legs from showing between his socks and his pants when he sat on the platform. Mother repaired to the bedroom to loosen the stays, straps, and hooks that held her figure in compliance with the limits of voluptuousness allowed Baptist preachers' wives in the fifties.

We had just had Sunday and we had *had* it. We had upheld the Word, done unto others, fed the five thousand, and won the day. Above all, we once again had passed the litmus test of Southern Baptist respectability. And if we didn't get things quite right that day, we had another go in seven days.

Regardless of how early my sister and I were awakened on Sunday morning, my father was dressed in his preaching clothes, ready to supervise the household until we left for the church.   He had already collected the *Dallas Morning News* from the front stoop and hidden it away from our temptation to dive into the funnies before church, an act that would not only reorder our priorities but throw off the Christian family's timely arrival at God's house for Sunday school.

Before leaving for church at nine-fifteen, we were expected to move about quietly so Dad could spend a few final moments on his sermon. Mother was absorbed in preparing a huge noon meal, practicing her opening comments to the women's Sunday school class she taught, and making sure that her seams were straight and her hat not perched antigoglin on her head.

Sandwiched between Mother's duties was her continuing battle with my sister and me over our choice of church attire—rejecting the sleeveless, the low-necked, the haltered, the gaudy-colored; the dangled earring and the jangling bracelet; the over-bright cheek, the barn-red lipstick, and—God forbid—the painted eye.   We were to look clean, demure, and virginal. The whole congregation would scrutinize the preacher's family for signs of latent humanity. The least we could do was to help Dad out on the job.

Certain rituals in the Baptist church were observed in Sunday School as if carved in stone. One of those was the opening assembly, where various groups met for a song, announcements, and a devotional before splitting off by age and gender into tiny enclosed areas lining the assembly hall.

Segregated in our cubicles, we were asked to turn in our offering envelopes, marked with the eight-point record system. The Baptist equivalent of the Spanish Inquisition, those eight points attested to godly behavior that week. As I remember, they were "Present," "On Time," "Bible Brought," "Lesson Prepared," "Daily Bible Reading," "Offering," "Prayer," and "Attend Church." After tallying our spiritual grades for the week, we reported on Visits and Letters/Cards/Phone Calls.

I always had problems with "On Time" since we were encouraged to fill out our envelopes at home and have them ready. I spent many an anxious moment on the way worrying about being late and having to lie or refigure my score.

My father believed in charging into morning worship on an up note, so we never commenced, as did many churches of that era, with folksy attendance reports from the Sunday school superintendent or the singing of "Happy Birthday" to various members of the congregation. At eleven o'clock sharp on a typical Sunday, the choir filed in; the ministers of education, music and the Word took up their stations in the pulpit; and a trumpet trio in the balcony burst forth with the fanfare to "God of Our Fathers." We sang all the verses with gusto, mindful that God was listening. Thus began the holiest hour of the week.

At noon, we often served lunch to official visitors—the revival evangelist, the furloughed missionary, the ministers of education and of music, or perhaps the summer youth director. It was a hot lunch with lots of gravy and congealed salads and homemade yeast rolls. When it was over, the women and girls retired to the kitchen to wash and dry the crystal, china, and silver, while the men settled in the living room to argue the latest moves of the Southern Baptist Convention or to account for the whereabouts of brethren they held in common acquaintance.

Then the lull fairy struck. About two, the visitors went away, and we children had to find something quiet to do for a couple of hours—at least until Dad went on his hospital visitation and Mother rose from her nap, renewed for the challenge of the second half of her day of rest.

During quiet time, my sister and I dallied about—read the funnies at last, scratched the dog's throat until he was beside himself with joy, polished our toenails, or took a discreet sunbath in the backyard. When "Omnibus" came on in 1951, I tuned the TV softly and sat near the screen. The safest things to do on Sunday afternoon were take a nap, make clever seasonal daily Bible reading reminders out of construction paper or egg cartons for Training Union, or study our Training Union parts.

Training Union, set for six-fifteen, was the evening twin of Sunday school. Not only did its timing prevent any extensive outings on Sunday afternoons, but it also kept a Baptist from being comfortable on Sunday night. One could not simply go to church in the evening, singing and praising God and listening while the preacher got all the *other* people told. No. Training Union had a life of its own, with lessons and "parts"—tortuous numbered paragraphs that were assigned in advance to be "given" by the hapless appointee. Reading one's part was a disgrace, showing the part giver had not cared enough for the things of the Spirit to spend an hour that sunny afternoon, with friends calling her to come out and play, to memorize her part.

On Sunday night we had to don again the scratchy tight hot things we wore Sunday morning. To wear a different outfit on Sunday night could bespeak materialism. It might also imply we had done something heathenishly athletic in the afternoon that provoked a rip or a stain in the day's original attire. (We wore our new Easter clothes the Sunday *before* or the Sunday *after* Easter. You figure it out.)

Through the age of fourteen, Training Union goers participated in an activity called the sword drill. Competitive and militaristic, this contest was designed to sharpen the ability of the participants to find scriptures quickly.

First, we drew sides and lined up facing each other with our Bibles clutched to our sides in the dominant hand. That was "At rest."

"Attention!" meant a West Point chin tuck and a heel click followed by complete silence.

"Draw Swords!" the leader would shout, and we whipped our Bibles level with our waists, one hand beneath the Bible and the other on top. At this time, there was a general casting about for anyone who might be sneakily edging his thumb toward the pages for a head start.

Next, the leader called out a Bible reference by book, chapter, and verse. Then the thumbs really got itchy, crooked high for Deuteronomy or stretched low for Revelation. A moment of silence followed—viciously long if the leader took pleasure in cruelty—

and then a repetition of the reference.   Another bit of sadistic silence and then "Charge!"

All hell broke loose as kids began slapping through God's Holy Word for the reference. Some crouched down and juggled the Bible on their knees to free both hands for pawing through it. Others staked out a foot prop, like the piano bench, and did a balancing act with the Bible on their raised knee. As soon as we found the reference, we stepped forward—marking the passage with a finger, bellies pooching out to support the weight of the Bible, feet slavishly together.

One last test validated the winner's accuracy. The smarty-pants got to read the verse. Of course, no one listened after the first word or two, but there was a chorus of howls if the initial words were in error. Then a fight followed about who tied for second.

To this day, I have to be careful in church not to call out "Charge!" when a reading is announced. It was a barbarous method of teaching children the canon of the Holy Word. And it worked. "Train up a child in the way he should go, and when he is old, he will not depart from it." That is Proverbs 22:6 and I found it in twelve seconds flat.

Everything about Sunday nights spelled completion. After the morning hymns castigating us as wretched sinners, worms, and strays, we were saved! saved! saved! in the evening song service. I sensed my parents' relief that another Sunday had not only been gotten through, it had been *achieved*—yea, executed, performed. My father had preached two or three times, shaken several hundred hands, visited the sick and afflicted, met with committees, and perhaps arbitrated a deacon fight.

Mother had taught a Sunday School class, played the piano for church, and dispensed gum and Kleenex during the sermon to one or two little ones temporarily orphaned by parents in the choir, her eyes all the while glazing at the thought of the roast seared and toughening in the oven at home. In the afternoon, she had, more than likely, sent flowers to a shut-in, prepared a plate of food for a tramp at the back door, answered the phone fourteen times, and readied for Training Union.

After evening worship, Mother laid out a feast of cold roast and turkey, rolls, pickled everything (peaches, okra, cucumbers), and whatever else she didn't want to start the new Christian week with. And we fell on the spread like junkyard dogs. "We" meant our family of four and a dozen or so others invited in for one reason or another: new church members, old ones moving away, lonely neighbors, friends, and a reprise of the evangelists, missionaries, and singers from the noon meal. There was talk— good, juicy church gossip, and a re-hash of each service ("Did you see that stray cat that came down the aisle on the first verse of the invitation?"—"Was he saved or had he come to re-dedicate his life?") And there were jokes, above all, jokes—told and re-told for new company.

We chased our leftovers with punch, angel food cake, and homemade ice cream, then sat around in the glow of a faith well-practiced. The infectious happiness of our parents spread to children and guests alike; we were caught up in our own little weekly Pentecost.

The tension of the evening invitation, with the pleading "every head bowed and every eye closed" was lifted and shelved until next Sunday. The saved were celebrated, the lost reassigned to God's keeping until next week—if they didn't by accident "go out into eternity tonight without Jesus."

When my sister and I hit our teens, Sunday nights changed considerably. Now we went to Youth Fellowship, a unique Baptist device designed to watch over the young folk from the time church ended, about 8:30, until 10:30, when we were expected home. After church, we reconvened in the home of some hapless church member who'd been asked to sponsor the fellowship that night (read "furnish food and disposable furniture to 25 howling adolescents"). We played charades and a game known as "Rhythm" where we clapped our number and someone else's in synch with the other clappers in the circle.

But of course the real games of Youth Fellowship went on in the courtship sector. Of paramount importance during evening worship was whether a certain person was going to fellowship. A number of pair-offs were accomplished during the fourth through sixth stanzas of "Just As I Am."

All sorts of subtle courtship gestures preoccupied the fellowshippers, from subtle knee touchings side by side on a couch to outright handholding. Sometimes the boy's arm got a cramp in it and he was forced to rest it on the back of the sofa, coincidentally touching the shoulders of the girl beside him.

The ride home, with couples in the back of the

sponsor's car, wallflowers riding shotgun to distract
the driver from glancing in the rearview mirror,
fortified the lovebirds with quick kisses and awkward
fumblings until next Sunday night's Fellowship, as
well as providing that week's go-togethers at school.

Boys were a little leery of me. I was first and
foremost the preacher's daughter, and they
apparently assumed any advance on me constituted a
one-way ticket to hell, via direct invitation of God or
my father. A few took up the challenge of the forbidden fruit. I remember one who whispered to me
one Sunday night in the back seat of the car, "What
would you do if I put my hand down your blouse?"
Another introduced me to long, slobbery kisses and
from then on, I was extremely ambiguous on the
matter of my body's being the temple of the
Holy Ghost.

In my early girlhood, there had been a good deal
of pulpiteering against any secular activities on
Sundays—household chores, cards, sports activities,
entertainment. We did not hang out clothes, iron,
sew, or wash cars on Sunday, much less dream of
going to the movies.

All that changed in the fifties. With the advent of
television, a mighty ambivalence descended. My
dad's favorite show came to be "What's My Line?"
which eventually aired at nine on Sunday nights. He
equivocated mightily at first, only watching out of the
corner of his eye, checking what he was allowing his
girls to see. But soon his love of words and the wit-
ticisms of John Daly, Dorothy Kilgallen, and Bennett
Cerf drew him in.

Then evening worship stopped promptly at 8:30.

The song service at the beginning was confined to
three or four rousers such as "There's Within My
Heart a Melody," "Love Lifted Me," and "Work, for
the Night is Coming." My father's sermons were
delivered without digression, and the invitation,
which formerly could be so long the old people had
to sit down and the young ones lean on the seat in
front for support, was now limited to three or four
whiny stanzas of "O, Why Not Tonight?" or "Softly
and Tenderly, Jesus is Calling."

But these concessions were not altogether the
harmless personal plottings of my father to indulge
himself in "What's My Line?" They were increasingly
a compromise to get people to come to church on
Sunday night at all. Everyone else wanted to be
home watching television also.

I have a hard time with Sundays now. I make it
fine until late afternoon. Then a restlessness sets in,
then a melancholy, and, unless I work at distracting
myself, a downright funk. (I have a friend who is
also regularly overtaken with blues for his lost
Sundays, and he says if he hears a dog whine mean-
ingfully, he can burst into tears mourning his Sunday
night Lassie.)

Though I could not have known it fully then, in
my own child's way, I must have sensed that Sunday
was our livelihood, that Sundays could make or
break us. And to Sunday went the grandest food,
the nicest clothes, the cleanest house, the most
cordiality, the happiest times. Sundays were so *filled*:
with the tension of Daddy's job, with the heavy
duties of respectability, with the joy of the saved and
the churched and the rededicated, with the horror of

the lost and the unregenerated and the backslidden.
Sunday was a great tide, swelling in the morning
with power and thrust and danger, receding in the
evening to relief and familial contentment.

I think I will not ever have heart's ease from the
sweetness and rue of those Texas Baptist Sundays.
Even today, the light of Sunday—the atmosphere, the
sunlight—is a different color to me from what it is
the rest of the week. Regardless of how many
furtive trips I make to Wal-Mart or H.E.B. on Sunday,
the day remains in my mind rife with godliness,
hallowed and set aside.

And in small, unobtrusive ways, I need to
perpetuate the roller-coaster Sunday atmosphere of
my childhood. Sundays I have to read. I have to
connect with my folks, retired now and back in
Waxahachie. I have to overeat. I have to make new
weekly resolutions. I have to go to church and sing
the hymns. I have to invent a party or find
something to laugh hysterically about. I have to
be quiet for a while.

There's one exception. I do not have to do a
sword drill.

To order HOMELAND by mail,
send $14 per copy

(includes shipping and applicable sales tax for Texas residents)

to:

New Santander Press
P.O. Box 306
Edinburg, Texas 78540